The Good Mood Kitchen

Also by Leslie Korn
Nutrition Essentials for Mental Health

Note:

The recipe for "Arugula–Fig–Peach Salad," the dish depicted on the cover of this book, can be found in the Good Mood Fruits section of Chapter 9.

The Good Mood Kitchen

Simple Recipes and Nutrition Tips for Emotional Balance

LESLIE KORN

W.W. Norton & Company
Independent Publishers Since 1923
New York • London

NOTE TO READERS: This book proposes to educate the reader about the role of diet and nutrition in mental health; neither the publisher nor the author(s) can guarantee the efficacy or appropriateness of any particular recommendation in every circumstance.

For information about permission to reproduce selections from this book, write to Permissions, W. W. Norton & Company, Inc., 500 Fifth Avenue, New York, NY 10110

For information about special discounts for bulk purchases, please contact W. W. Norton Special Sales at specialsales@wwnorton.com or 800-233-4830

Manufacturing by Edwards Brothers Malloy
Book design by Vicki Fischman
Production manager: Christine Critelli

Library of Congress Cataloging-in-Publication Data

Names: Korn, Leslie E., author.
Title: The good mood kitchen : simple recipes and nutrition tips for
    emotional balance / Leslie Korn.
Description: New York : W.W. Norton & Company, [2017] | Includes
    bibliographical references and index.
Identifiers: LCCN 2017014287 | ISBN 9780393712223 (hardcover)
Subjects: LCSH: Mental health—Nutritional aspects. | Cooking.
Classification: LCC RC455.4.N8 K66 2017 | DDC 641.5/63—dc23
LC record available at https://lccn.loc.gov/2017014287

W. W. Norton & Company, Inc.,
500 Fifth Avenue, New York, N.Y. 10110
www.wwnorton.com

W. W. Norton & Company Ltd.,
15 Carlisle Street, London W1D 3BS

1 2 3 4 5 6 7 8 9 0

For my husband, Rudolph Rÿser,
who has taught me so much about food and cooking—co-forager,
cooking partner, and "good mood" role model.

Contents

Acknowledgments

There are many people in my life, present and past, to whom I owe a debt of gratitude for their contributions to my own "good mood," as well as my professional work. Of these many, four are foremost in my mind and heart. My exploration of the role of culture, foods, and medicine began in early life with my grandmothers, Jessica Schindler Finberg and Esther Hirsch Korn, who cooked sumptuous old-country meals reflecting their wisdom about nourishment. In my professional studies, no one has influenced my work in nutrition and diet more than the late Dr. Nicholas Gonzalez, a brilliant and generous physician who is the reason why I, a 27 years-long vegetarian, am now a "recovered vegetarian." We lost Nick too soon, but I hope that this book contributes a small portion to his legacy. Finally, I would like to thank my editor at Norton, Benjamin Yarling, whose consistent enthusiasm for our collaboration brings out my best, and for that I am ever thankful.

The Good Mood Kitchen

PART 1

Welcome to the Good Mood Kitchen

CHAPTER 1

What Is Mood-Savvy Nutrition?

There is no doubt that nutrition affects mental health. Poor nutrition leads to and exacerbates mental illness. Optimal nutrition prevents and treats mental illness. Note the word "optimal" to describe nutrition that prevents and treats illness. One's diet cannot be just "good," or providing the basics for survival; it must be nutrient dense and tailored to the needs of the individual, who may have been missing the basic ingredients for optimal brain function since life in the womb.

Where there is mental illness, there is very often poor diet. Where there is mental illness, there is usually a long history of digestive problems. By adding the lens of nutrition, diet, and digestion to your personal toolbox, you can forever change your approach to self-care and enhance the efficacy of your eating habits for optimal energy, health, and emotional well-being.

I have written this book to take you step by step through all the essentials required to revolutionize your personal diet with mental health-savvy recipes and tips. Even if you do not apply all of these approaches yourself, this is an opportunity to explore food substitutions, eating principles, and recipes that will, without a doubt, enhance your well-being and stamina.

Changing your thoughts, beliefs, behaviors, and habits can be challenging. It happens slowly. Changing nutritional beliefs and behaviors is no different from changing other beliefs and behaviors, but results are assured. This book is not ideological; it is practical in that it provides concrete steps to modify your eating behaviors for healthful results.

Knowing who you are and what your body needs is the art and science of mental health nutrition. Some people function best as carnivores, others function better as vegetarians. But what is incontrovertible is that nutrition matters. It is the most important missing link to mental health in society today.

In the chapters that follow, I will guide you through each stage of dietary and nutritional change. I will suggest some first steps, but nutritional change is much like a jigsaw puzzle. No matter where you start, you'll begin to discover new patterns that lead to improved health.

When discussing diet and nutrition with the people I work with in my professional practice, I usually suggest that they use a food, mood, and exercise diary, which asks them to keep detailed track for three days of what they eat, how they feel, and when they move or exercise. I'd like to recommend this practice to you, too. The food diary is a valuable tool for taking stock of your current self-care routines—or lack of them—and can greatly enhance awareness of what you're eating and how it's affecting your energy and mood. However the conversation begins, recognizing that mood is a mind-body experience and not just based on personal history or mental processes can be crucial in enhancing your sense of self-efficacy, feeling empowered and motivated to take action, and broadening your perspective on the many pathways to change.

CHAPTER 2

Where to Start

If, as the act of picking this book up suggests, you're ready to start making changes to feel better physically, mentally, and emotionally, and to have more fun in the kitchen, you might ask yourself: "What do I do first?"

I've listed below some questions to ask yourself, both now and as you continue to read and learn about mood-savvy nutrition in ways that can add to and inform the way you cook and eat. There's plenty to learn, but there's no correct or incorrect way to make changes. You can start right away, and then continue to adapt and expand as you learn more over the course of this book.

What is essential when making changes is to make the changes you feel like making first and that you will feel successful doing. I encourage you to ask the following questions of yourself now, and write the answers down, as a helpful way to begin exploring your diet, your eating behaviors, and the food-mood connections you experience:

- How many of my meals am I preparing?
- How many meals a week are "fast food?"
- How am I preparing my meals?
- Which foods make me feel good?
- Which foods make me feel bad?
- How do foods alter my consciousness?
- What foods do I like but don't often prepare?
- Who are my allies for changing my diet in the family?
- Who are my allies for changing my diet among my friends?

Another exercise I'd suggest as a way of initiating your movement toward a mood-savvy diet is to make a food substitution list so that you can gradually substitute healthy foods for unhealthy ones without sacrificing any pleasure in eating. You can base your personal substitution list on the one I've provided, or custom-build your own as you continue to read and learn about the nutrition essentials of mental health.

Always remember this: The change process can be slow, so be gentle with yourself. While a pinch of self-discipline (or discipline from an encouraging friend or partner) is always useful, you don't need to use too heavy a hand. Gentle self-compassion is the key to long-term success.

Above all, remember to "trust your gut" as you embark on this adventure. We explore in the next chapter how the "gut" affects everything—from the food we digest, to what nourishes our brain and body, as well as our emotional well-being.

Building on our concept of substituting healthy foods for unhealthy ones but still satisfying our needs, try this exercise. Using two columns, make a list of the foods that comfort you in the left column. As you review these foods, make another list of healthy substitutions for these foods in the right column. I have started you off with some examples. You fill in the rest.

Maintain a Food Substitutions List	
Comfort foods you enjoy	Healthy substitutions
Wheat toast with butter and jam	Baked potato with butter, organic sour cream, and real bacon bits or chives
Fast-food French fries	Potatoes or yuca baked in olive oil and topped with cilantro mayonnaise dip
Sugary soft drinks	Sparling water with fresh berries and stevia

As you consider making positive changes for your mental and physical well-being, consider the ways in which you can enjoy the process, and have fun and be creative. If change becomes difficult or boring, or begins to feel unattainable, then you will not feel successful and achieve your goals. Engage your family, friends, and health providers for support as you explore this journey toward feeling better each day.

MAKING CHANGE HAPPEN

Now, try answering the following questions. You can do this alone or with those whom you regularly share meals with. If you do this process with family or friends, make sure that you fill out your answers privately first; then come together over a healthy potluck meal to compare answers and find areas where you can share goals and support each other through obstacles.

- Identify three positive overall changes you want to achieve (such as more energy, more stable mood, less irritability, less pain).
- Name three new positive behaviors to incorporate, in order of importance.
- Name three negative habits to release, in order of importance.
- Identify at least one addictive food to release—or more to be released, one at a time.
- Name three food substitutions that are satisfying.
- Identify your three strengths, and list three possible obstacles.
- Name three ways you will have fun and be creative in this change process.
- What is the phrase that will remind you to practice self-compassion?

OVERCOMING THE ADDICTION TO FAST FOOD

Later in the book you'll make a list of three foods you feel addicted to and wish to reduce or eliminate from your diet. As you continue to read and learn about the key ingredients of mood-savvy cooking and eating, think about the following questions, and consider how they apply to foods you wish to avoid:

- How often do you eat this food?
- How often would you like to eat this food?
- What will be the benefits of reducing or eliminating this food?
- What will be the challenges?
- What foods will serve as satisfactory substitutions?

Below, for a jump-start, is a list of common food addictions and suggested alternatives.

Common Food Addictions and Suggested Alternatives	
Wheat	Gluten-free flour, breads, and other products
Sugar	Honey, stevia, or agave nectar
Milk chocolate with sugar	Dark chocolate sweetened with stevia
Soda pop	Sparkling water mixed with fresh fruit or sugar-free juice and stevia
Coffee/caffeine	Green tea, matcha, yerba maté, roasted dandelion root, Rhodiola tea, ramón nut coffee (café de capomo)
Table salt	Sea salt, seaweed flakes, herbal mixtures
Fast food	Slow food; crock pot food; fast food made like slow food, such as organic hotdogs with fresh sauerkraut; homemade tacos with blue corn tortillas, fresh chopped and sautéed meat, pinto beans and raw cabbage and fresh salsa
Bottled salsa and chips fried in corn oil	Fresh diced tomato, cilantro, onion, jalapeño, with fresh avocado and fresh tortillas lightly fried in olive or coconut oil

CRAVINGS

When people are addicted to fast foods, such as those containing high sugars and high salt levels, they become inured to taste and lose the ability to taste foods in their natural state.

Mood affects food cravings, and food cravings also affect mood. Cravings are complex and may derive from several causes. Understanding the foods, the time of day, the food-as-self-medication factor, food allergies, and mood prior to cravings is essential and can be reviewed during the assessment process.

There are several factors that contribute to food cravings:

• Nutrient deficits may cause people to crave food with nutrients they need. This is "cravings as self-medication."

- Specific foods are formulated to be addictive and lead to cravings, especially processed foods. This is "cravings as addiction."
- Foods that people are allergic to can cause cravings for those foods; this is "cravings as allergy/sensitivity."

TIPS FOR DEALING WITH FOOD CRAVINGS

- Reduce stress to help avoid the tendency to reach for addictive substances as a coping mechanism.
- Keep addictive foods out of sight to help keep them out of your mind.
- Identify foods that precede or trigger your cravings, and avoid them.
- Engage in alternative strategies for your attention, such as computer games, relaxation, and exercise.
- Drink water throughout the day.
- When a craving is for a comfort food not in alignment with your diet goals, substitute something healthy instead.
- Just rinsing the mouth with starchy carbohydrates triggers brain response and increases energy.
- Plan "snacks ahead" so if you grab something, it is healthier but satisfying.
- Allow some compassion for your cravings, but in small portions; for example, allow craving responses twice a week but not every night.

NUTRIENT SUPPLEMENTATION FOR REDUCING CRAVINGS

- Vitamin B complex is useful in raising serotonin levels, thus improving mood and the body's ability to metabolize carbohydrates.
- Chromium and L-glutamine both help to regulate blood sugar levels and can reduce cravings for carbohydrates and sugars.
- Fish oil helps to reduce cravings for sugar by enhancing insulin sensitivity.
- L-tyrosine supports the production of dopamine that contributes to improving mood.

- Magnesium is useful in reducing stress, balancing blood sugar, and improving sleep.
- DL-phenylalanine increases endorphin levels, and tryptophan raises serotonin levels and reduces cravings for carbohydrates.

DID YOU KNOW?

The HAPIfork

The HAPIfork is a biofeedback, electronic fork that helps you monitor and track your eating habits. It also alerts you with the help of indicator lights and gentle vibrations when you are eating too fast. Every time you bring food from your plate to your mouth with your fork, this action is called a "fork serving." The HAPIfork also measures:

- How long it took to eat your meal
- The amount of "fork servings" taken per minute
- Intervals between "fork servings"

BE YOUR OWN COACH: TIPS FOR SUCCESS

- Give yourself pep talks, talk back to yourself, and boost yourself when you lag.
- Know thyself: Don't do "what works for others." Explore deeply within to clarify what works for you.
- If you are the type of person who benefits from "quick changes," then begin with a change that you will feel quickly so you feel successful—like a high-protein, low-carbohydrate diet for 7 days to stabilize blood sugar.
- Try not to get too tired or hungry.
- Incorporate mindfulness—a compassionate, moment-to-moment approach to change.
- Use mindfulness to balance goals for change with a "no goals" approach.
- Listen to your gut.
- Focus on what you want to eat and can eat for health, not what you cannot.

- Engage your family and friends for support.
- Give yourself a "break." Others do, why not you?
- Start with where you will observe the fastest and most important changes first.
- Start slowly and build according to your success.
- Balance the use of vitamins, minerals, botanicals, and glandulars.
- Review and change your approach every 3 months.
- Combine nutrients where possible to include powders and liquids or reduce the number of pills and capsules required.

PLATES AND COLORS

The size and color of dinnerware affect how much you eat. Smaller plates reduce portion size. Colors that contrast the food on the plate will help you to eat less, and plate colors that match the food will help you to eat more. Tablecloths with a low contrast to plate color will reduce the desire to overeat (Van Ittersum & Wansink, 2012).

MANAGING COSTS

Most nutritional products that are sold at retail prices are generally marked up by 100% of the wholesale price. Coordinate with a nonprofit purchasing cooperative, a wholesale club, or tribal clinics and pharmacies to secure the high quality at a lower cost.

MONEY-SAVING SHOPPING
AND FOOD-BUYING TIPS

- Join a community-supported agriculture (CSA) program, or volunteer at a co-op or farm and get reduced prices.
- Look for day-old bins at the supermarket, which often have vegetables that make good soups.
- Shop on the perimeter of the supermarket, where you will most often find healthy food.
- Buy in bulk.

- Buy bones and cheap cuts of organic meat for flavoring and making broths for soups and to sauté.
- Buy fresh produce in season, when it is lowest in price.
- Shop at ethnic food stores, where they often have less expensive herbs, fresh roots, and low farm-to-store pricing, including Mexican, Asian, and Indian stores, for example.
- Buy frozen foods like berries to save money and retain quality.
- Shop to prepare meals in which half of your plate is fruits and vegetables.
- Look for leafy greens like kale, chard, collards, spinach, and broccoli, which are some of the most nutritious, least expensive foods you can buy.
- Purchase canned salmon, sardines (boneless, skinless), smoked mackerel, and anchovies, which are inexpensive alternatives to fresh fish.
- Avoid packaged or canned food that has more than four ingredients on the label.

Planning meals by writing up a grocery list in advance will save money and time. There are numerous useful and easy-to-use apps for the computer or other instruments, such as "Cooksmarts," which helps with meal planning and recipes. Some basic principles of meal planning are outlined next.

MEAL PLANNING

1. Create a list of your family's favorite recipes and make sure they are easily accessible, whether in cookbooks or bookmarked on your browser.
2. Clean and organize your freezer, because you will need to make room for leftovers. Having glass storage containers and glass baking dishes will come in handy for storing leftovers. Plastic freezer bags are also useful.
3. Keep track of items that you are running low on or that you need to restock in your cupboards. A magnetized whiteboard on the fridge can be quite handy for this, or even a notepad that you keep in the kitchen. Be sure to bring this list with you when you go to the store. At the end of the book I provide you with checklists to use and adapt.
4. Record the meals that you will be cooking during the week,

using a calendar in the kitchen, a day planner, or a magnetized whiteboard. Use it to make notes about what you may need to do in advance, like thawing or marinating meat.

5. Consider planning the other meals for each day of the week—in addition to dinner—including snacks.

6. Create your list before going to the store. Look at your favorite recipes and pick out which ones you want to cook for the week. Write down everything that you will need. Make columns for different parts of the store and list the ingredients that you will need from each one. For instance, use columns for produce, bulk, dairy, meat, and frozen food. Make sure to shop with a full belly, to help you avoid impulse buying or getting more than you need.

7. Save peelings from vegetables in a tub in the fridge during the week, so you can add them to your vegetable broth.

MAKING TIME

A common reason that we do not prepare healthy food is because we do not think we have enough time to cook. Preparing a large, healthy meal on the weekend and cooking enough so that there are leftovers is one way to ensure that there is healthy food available during busy times. Meals that freeze well include broth-based soups and casseroles. When making a casserole, double the recipe and freeze the extra in small meal-size containers that can be defrosted and warmed on another day.

Plan and Prep a Week at a Time

1. Pick a day of the week to organize food and food preparation for the week. For example, many of the basics can be prepared on a Sunday, for example, and will last the week.

2. Roast one chicken—eat half on Sunday night and the other half can be boned and prepared as a chicken salad for lunch. Add the leftover bones to the bone broth pot. Make a Crock-Pot chicken soup from another chicken, adding vegetables, onions, and garlic, then strain the broth and use as a base for preparing rice or as a soup later in the week, and bone the chicken and store for later in the week or as a snack.

3. Involve the family in cooking, or plan a potluck or food exchange with friends. If you are making soup, make a double batch and trade it with a friend who is making another soup or casserole.

4. When beginning to cook a meal, think ahead for the next few meals and take any preparation methods into account, such as soaking legumes or nuts, or marinating meat.

5. Wash and prepare your vegetables for the week to have them ready for easy use in cooking or for snacking. Include carrots, celery, broccoli, lettuce, bell peppers, mushrooms, zucchini, and so on.

6. Gather all the vegetables you want for salads and prepare raw salads in jars for 3–4 days at a time.

7. Make a vegetable broth rich in potassium by placing all the stems and ends of vegetables in a Crock-Pot.

8. Peel large amounts of garlic, place whole bulbs in the oven, and bake at 300 degrees Fahrenheit until the individual cloves open. Remove from the oven and pull apart the individual cloves.

9. Use a Crock-Pot in which you place all your meat bones for bone broth.

10. Fill a baking tray with sweet potatoes and bake them; then store them in the fridge. They can be sliced and eaten cold, made into a custard as a dessert, or reheated and topped with butter, sliced, and pan-fried quickly in butter and balsamic vinegar.

11. Steam beets and store them in the fridge; you can add yogurt and eat them as a snack, or eat them sliced over salad.

12. Prepare 2–3 salad dressings, choosing from among the recipes in the Recipe Index section at the end of the book, and store them in bottles in the fridge.

13. Prepare several cups of brown rice or another grain, which can be reheated and added to soups or stir-fried as needed throughout the week.

14. Soak almonds and raisins—cover almonds and raisins with water and place them in Tupperware. Let it sit overnight. Use as needed.

15. Place a cheese slice and a hard-boiled egg together in a Tupperware container for an easy protein snack.
16. Put bone broth in a thermos to have it available throughout the day.

TRAVELING WITH COOLER BAGS AND THERMOSES

Having cooler bags with you when you travel allows you to buy healthy foods that are easy to eat on the road, rather than relying on fast food and restaurants for your meals. Fill baggies with water and freeze them, and then use these as freezer packs to keep things cool. Good travel foods include hard-boiled eggs; dried fruit and nuts; fresh fruit and raw vegetables; aged hard cheese; gluten-free or whole grain crackers; canned Pacific wild salmon, sardines, or anchovies; water in glass bottles; olive oil and vinegar to add to salads; a Tupperware filled with fresh greens; Kombucha or herbal beverage in glass bottles; and almond butter.

TIPS FOR TRAVELING AND EATING WHILE ON VACATION

1. Avoid high-carbohydrate foods at breakfast and opt for simple protein foods like fried eggs and bacon (note that at hotels and buffets most scrambled eggs come from a premade egg mix and sausage meat has additives, so choose the fruit and hard-boiled eggs when possible, and avoid the pastries).
2. Order salad with grilled meat for lunch and ask for simple dressings like olive oil and vinegar or lemon. Restaurants will usually have it in the kitchen.
3. Choose proteins that are less likely to be mass produced, like venison, bison, or lamb, and choose wild-caught fish (preferably from Alaska).
4. Avoid soups in restaurants as they are usually made with broths high in wheat and monosodium glutamate (MSG).
5. Travel with a small supply of energy bars, almonds, rice cakes, almond butter, hard-boiled eggs, and canned sardines—to carry you over until you can get to a store.
6. If staying with family, you can buy groceries to contribute healthy options to meals.

MOOD-SAVVY EATING AT RESTAURANTS

- Go to a restaurant with plenty of healthy attitude. Don't be afraid to ask questions and request what you need. Don't feel shy asking about food quality when with your friends or family. You are a role model for self-care when you demand quality food.
- Make your own healthy salad dressing: Carry your own small bottle of virgin olive oil or ask the waitperson.
- Ask them to hold the salt in your food: Most restaurants use table salt, which is not a healthy condiment. Carry your own sea salt if you want salt on your food.
- Order outside of the menu. Ask for a plate of steamed veggies or food made to your specifications. Many restaurants will honor your request.
- If ordering fish, ask if it's wild or farmed. Most of the time it's farmed.
- Ask if the soups or sauces are made with flour; if so, they have gluten.
- Ask for milk or cream (not creamer or half-n-half) or better yet, forgo it as it's often poor-quality dairy.
- Ask for real butter, instead of margarine or butter substitutes.
- It is common in restaurants and hotels for "fake" egg mixtures to be served as scrambled eggs. Ask for real eggs, poached or hard-boiled, to be made for you.
- Pancakes are often served with fake maple syrup. If they do not have the real syrup and if you eat this meal, ask for a little honey instead.
- Avoid drinks like premade iced tea. They are made from powders and sugar. Ask for an herbal tea and a glass with ice and make your healthy iced tea at the table.
- Many lower-quality restaurants serve premade soups, sauces, and frozen foods. Ask about whether a soup is premixed. Ask if a sauce is premixed. Many dishes served as fish or breaded are really frozen and deep-fried. Avoid these.
- Best practice! It's worth going to a better-quality restaurant occasionally where foods are fresh, natural, and made daily.

- Eat a healthy snack and drink a glass of water before you go out to eat. You will spend less and also be less inclined to eat poor-quality food.
- Avoid buffets; the food is often poor quality and prone to bacteria, and buffets encourage overeating.
- When eating at restaurants serving soy sauce, ask for reduced-sodium soy sauce. If you have a gluten sensitivity, ask for tamari (wheat-free soy sauce), or bring your own.
- Ask for sauces to be served on the side, so you can determine how much to use.

Restaurants will often be difficult for those with multiple food allergies. One solution is to find the most compatible option on the menu, and then ask about substitutions to create an option that works for you. The relationship between good nutrition and whole, fresh foods prepared with slow or minimal processing is unquestionable. But where do you begin? For many foods, the least amount of processing (raw) ensures the maximum nutrition and healthful benefits, while for others a long slow cook or a quick steam is best. Slow cooking in water, boiling, salting, broiling, pickling, roasting, baking, drying, steaming, fermenting, and smoking are the preferable processing methods that ensure maximum nutrition. Frying, deep-fat frying, high-temperature cooking, and preserving with nitrates and nitrites are the most injurious methods and contribute to poor mental and physical health.

ELIMINATING MICROWAVE USE

Microwaves alter the molecular structure of food and hence its nutritional benefits; therefore, microwave ovens should never be used to prepare food. Microwaves produce unnatural molecules in food and transform other molecules and amino acids into toxic and carcinogenic forms. However, microwaves are not without value; the "lazy Susan" plate inside your microwave makes it ideal for the storage of spice and herb bottles.

CROCK-POT

If you have only one appliance in the kitchen, it should be the versatile Crock-Pot. Crock-Pot cooking is one of the best ways to introduce cooking to someone who does not cook or who does not have a lot of time to cook. Using a Crock-Pot is inexpensive, and slow-cooking foods—especially bones, meats, and legumes—at low temperatures is the best way to retain nutrients. Always use unsalted butter and sea salt when cooking with the Crock-Pot, and be sure to put meat juices back into sauces and stews—they are rich in "happiness" amino acids.

BLENDER

A blender is the next appliance to buy for making smoothies, sauces, and dressings. A high-speed blender is the best option, as the typical household blender does not have the ability to process hard foods like nuts and seeds, and will not produce as smooth a liquid.

MOOD-SAVVY KITCHEN EQUIPMENT

Begin with the items in this list. Buy stainless steel, enamel, or glass pots. Avoid aluminum and nonstick items as they can emit toxins. Build your collection by asking for kitchenware for gifts when you have a special gift-giving event.

- Slow cooker
- Steamer pot
- 2 knives: a paring knife and a large chopping knife
- Blender or immersion blender for smoothies
- Pots for boiling eggs or making soup
- Fry pan
- Strainer
- Colander
- Cutting board
- Spatula
- Soup ladle
- 2-cup measuring cup
- Oven mitt or pot holder

Over time, add these items:

- Juice extractor
- Grater/zester
- Spiralizer
- Food processor
- Small, medium, and large, glass baking dishes
- Mixing bowls
- Cast-iron skillet
- Coffee grinder for grinding coffee as well as spices

NUTRITIONAL CHANGE FOR COUPLES AND FAMILIES

Mindful eating extends to couples, families, and group activity as well. Even the simple though often forgotten act of eating together as a family while sharing news of the day leads to reduction of weight gain when compared to meals spent watching TV. How do we get children to participate in healthy nutritional and behavioral changes?

Beginning at age 4, children are at a good age to start helping in the kitchen. Cooking together is fun and involves building skills, including learning math and measurements, geography, chemistry, and nutrition, along with patience and teamwork. If your child is studying something in school, why not plan a theme dinner around that geographic location and include ethnic cuisine and invite one of her or his friends, or their family, to participate? The skill of cooking is becoming a lost art, and equipping your child to cook is a lasting healthy gift. For example, you could have tamale-making night; in addition to the fun group effort, it is an opportunity to talk about tamales and where corn is from, where salsas and chilies are from, as well as coconut and chocolate. Younger children can learn to count by measuring, and to practice their reading skills by reading recipes.

COOKING WITH KIDS

- Take children shopping, so they can help pick ingredients.
- Have healthy snacks in easy-to-reach places for kids, to encourage healthy eating.

- Make cooking fun and exciting, to encourage them—play music, have a conversation.
- Make a list of activities for children to help with in the kitchen.
- Make yogurt.
- Make sprouts and watch them grow.
- Plant wheat berries and watch them grow into wheatgrass.
- Make healthy cupcakes.
- Measure ingredients.
- Make healthy Almond Joys.
- Make smoothies.
- Make sauerkraut and then put it on hot dogs.
- Make gluten-free pizza dough and then have a pizza party.
- Use a spiralizer; they are a lot of fun.

COMMUNITY-SUPPORTED AGRICULTURE AND HOME GARDENS

Many regions have community-supported agriculture (CSA) programs. These are local food production farms that also have a centralized area of distribution in urban settings. Volunteering on a farm during the summer brings cost down, and many of these farms also engage in humane animal husbandry, which can supply quality animal-based proteins. Starting a home garden, or setting up an herbal kitchen with culinary herbs, or just exploring the use of herbal roots and leaves can be an important start for making changes.

NUTRITIONAL CHANGE TAKES TIME

It is natural that we want change to be fast, and we are conditioned to expect this by the promise of fast-acting medications and advertisements. But fast acting often brings side effects. Depression, anxiety, post-traumatic stress disorder (PTSD), insomnia, and addictions develop over years; the causes have been in place for a while, and it will take time to restore and recover balance. So be patient with yourself and the process.

AN IMAGE FOR HEALTHY CHANGE

Consider the following image for your process, or create one of your own: A tree grows slowly, but surely, digging roots into the earth for stability as it spreads its branches and leaves to the sky. The roots absorb water from below and the leaves from above. Nourishment comes from many directions. There are many roots and branches and leaves, and over time the tree becomes fuller and stronger. This slow but sure approach promises success, so that when a wind blows, the tree does not topple over easily but moves with the wind. This is the process of nature and savvy, good mood nutrition.

Change takes place by first integrating positive activities—which soon become habits—and then eliminating negative activities and habits. Practically, this means a step-by-step approach to identify one positive behavior that will change or replace a negative behavior, and employing the principle of substitutions outlined in this book.

Focus on the specific actions that will improve your well-being based on the goals you have identified, and above all have fun and share the process with your family and friends.

CHAPTER 3

How Good Mood Meals Work

With just a small amount of background knowledge, even those with no prior familiarity with the role of nutrition in mood balance and mental health can improve their eating habits and take positive new steps for more sustained health and emotional balance. I've outlined the key principles you need to know below.

SAY YES TO ANCESTRAL DIETS

One of the points I emphasize throughout this book is the concept of "traditional nutrition and foods." These are foods, diets, and preparation methods that have been used by our ancestors for millennia. They are foods that have evolved to optimize nourishment. In modern society, which usually follows the standard American diet (SAD), food and diet are often dissociated from authentic cultural traditions.

We are, however, experiencing revitalization across modern SAD societies of reclaiming local, fresh, nutrient-dense, and optimally prepared traditional foods made relevant to our needs for the 21st century.

In this book I explain low-cost approaches to mental health nutrition. As you will see, food is much more than nourishment: Food is medicine; food is nutrition; food is ceremonial; food is sacred; food is culture and tradition; food is an anchor to culture and personal well-being.

The traditional nutrition—also called *authentic* or *ancestral nutrition*—approach to mental health suggests that in order to achieve health and well-being, mentally and physically, we should eat the types of foods that are similar to the foods our ancestors ate. This means foods free of refined sugars and grains—minimally processed—with no synthetic preservatives or food coloring. These foods should be prepared in their natural state. Traditional or authentic foods are low glycemic, anti-inflammatory, and rich in omega-3 fatty acids. Depending on the region of the world, traditional foods may include a low-to-moderate or even high complex carbohydrate, moderate-protein, moderate- to high-fat diet. These foods include antioxidant-rich fruits and vegetables of all colors, as well as fiber sources—also known as prebiotics—which may include bark flour, psyllium, chia, cactus, bran, and oatmeal. Fermented foods such as kimchi, sauerkraut, and fresh natural yogurt and kefir provide probiotics for digestion, colon health, and detoxification.

There is a tremendous diversity of foods available, and we have the ability to adapt and use many foods of our neighbors as well as ancestors. Some of our ancestors ate a diet of fresh blood and raw milk (and still do); others ate lots of blubber and fish and only a few carbohydrates in the forms of berries and roots during the summer months. Traditional diets obtain dietary fats from fish, birds, plants, and wild game. Wild animals have only one-tenth the fat of farmed cattle, include natural essential fatty acids, and they also do not have the harmful antibiotics and hormones that disrupt endocrine function and gut health.

The prominent dentist Dr. Weston Price, in the course of his global travels in traditional societies, researched the question: "Who is the healthiest among peoples on the planet?" While looking for an answer, he found that the healthiest societies in the world consumed moderate amounts of saturated and monounsaturated animal fats, suggesting that our modern fears of saturated fats are among the myths of modern medicine. He and other researchers also failed to find any society that was *vegan*, which suggests that veganism is a modern dietary invention and while there is much emotional and spiritual merit in veganism, there is little evidence for any biological merit.

Authentic foods are those foods and medicines that naturally evolved over time within a specific human culture. These foods bring balance to the body, mind, and spirit. How does one integrate authentic foods, traditional foods, and whole foods today while living in rural or urban settings? What are the options for using food as a delicious source of nutrition and medicine?

As a general rule we all benefit when the majority of our daily food intake includes whole foods that are nutrient dense and freshly prepared. Some proportion of daily food should include both raw and cooked foods, and ideally some wild foods. Food that is obtained from cans or other packages should be minimized. Slow cooking in water, boiling, salting, broiling, pickling, roasting, baking, drying, steaming, fermenting, and some smoking are the essential processing methods that ensure maximum nutrition. Frying should be limited to special occasions. By preparing fresh foods, one can control the preparation, including the amount of salt and commercial fats used, in order to maintain optimal nutritional value. Fresh foods are also free of harmful preservatives.

One of the most important principles in successful mood-savvy nutrition is that there is no one diet for everyone. For nutrition to be effective, diet must be tailored to the metabolism of each individual. Nutritional needs are determined biochemically at the individual level. This is genetically based and is culturally and environmentally linked to our ancestry. Aligning our "fuel" with the rate at which we can burn it enhances efficiency and performance. A consistent use of fuel inappropriate for the individual body leads to decline.

SAY NO TO THE STANDARD AMERICAN DIET

The standard American diet (SAD) makes us sad! This too-frequently followed diet consists of refined, overly processed foods containing refined sugars in fruit juices and sugary drinks, and highly refined rice, pastas, and flours used in breads and bakery goods. These processed products are loaded with chemicals and synthetic preservatives, hormones, antibiotics, and food colorings that are known to alter our mood. This type of diet is a prime contributing factor in common mood and mental health challenges. The SAD leads to chronic inflammatory states and sets the stage for neurotransmitter imbalances.

The SAD diet makes us *sad* because it does not provide the nutrients our brain and body need to function well. That some of us survive (though rarely thrive) on a SAD diet is just the luck of the draw. For some people the resulting illness comes in childhood; for others it doesn't show up until middle age. But it invariably comes, just as a car without the right fuel eventually sputters to a stop.

There are many reasons why people do not receive the nourishment their minds/bodies need. Many experience chronic poverty or injury-related economic loss that precludes access to high-quality, nutritious food. Some simply do not know much about good nutrition. Many people may be addicted to substances such as alcohol, cocaine, or methamphetamines and, as a result, do not eat well or enough, and do not properly metabolize what they do eat. Pharmaceutical medications, alcohol, and many commercially produced drugs deplete important nutrients needed by the body. The list goes on; but there is a solution.

SAY YES TO INDIVIDUALIZED NUTRITION

One helpful way to think about taking an individualized approach to your diet and nutrition is to use the metaphor of a car. Different kinds of vehicles require different kinds of gas. For example, if I put 87-octane fuel into a car that takes only diesel, I can destroy the engine. Some cars do better with lower octane and some higher octane; the right fuel ensures the smooth running of the vehicle. This does not always mean that a vehicle will not run, but more that it will not run optimally in the way it is meant to.

The importance of using the right gas for a car is analogous to how we treat our own "engine." Each of us has an engine that requires a different mix of "fuel." Fuel in the form of food is made up of protein, carbohydrates, and fats. The correct fuel mix, meaning the correct ratio of protein, carbohydrates, and fats for the individual will ensure smooth healthy functioning. The concept that a healthy diet must be adapted to the individual, which is based in science, thus sheds light on all the confusion about the various diets that are out there and also the confusion about research on diets, all of which can show both positive effects and negative effects. It is not the diet that determines well-being, but the individual's alignment with the dietary "fuel." To continue the analogy between a car's fuel—and the combustion that moves it forward—and human fuel, such as food, then what we are looking at scientifically is called *oxidation*. Oxidation is the rate at which we burn carbohydrates, or glucose. Some of us burn carbohydrates more quickly, and some burn them more slowly; the speed at which we burn carbohydrates can be considered our nutritional type.

Let's continue the car metaphor to examine the body-mind connections involved in our dietary choices: Daily, one has to ensure the engine (the brain-digestive system) has the proper fuel mix (carbohydrates, proteins, and fats). If the octane is too low, there's backfiring (fermentation and gas). If it is too high, it goes unused and is a waste, leaving waste deposits (gout). At periodic intervals one has to change the oil filter (flush the gallbladder), tune the engine (take a rest), do a lube (ingest fish oils or hydrate), and of course wash the car (detoxify).

A car may perform well when it is new (young), but as it reaches the 50,000-mile mark (40–50 years) it begins to break down—if it hasn't already. The clutch goes, the brakes give out, and under extreme stress, such as cold wet winters, the bottom rusts out (adrenal foundation) and the paint (skin) cracks. The truth is that people often take better care of their cars than their bodies!

LEARN WHAT TYPE OF OXIDIZER YOU ARE

People can be divided into three general body categories:

- *Fast oxidizers,* whose blood pH tends toward a little more acid and who are carnivores
- *Mixed or balanced individuals* who do well with a mix of carbohydrates, proteins, and fats
- *Slow oxidizers,* whose blood pH tends to be more alkaline and who do better on more plant proteins

What foods/fuel mix we require is determined by our genetics, just like the color of our eyes, our height, or our blood type. We are a product of our parents' rates of oxidation, also called metabolism. If we are eating food that does not burn efficiently based on the needs of our engine, then we will not function optimally, and this also underlies not only physical but mental health challenges.

HOW TO IDENTIFY YOUR OXIDIZER TYPE

NIACIN TEST: Take 50 mg of niacin on an empty stomach. Niacin creates a strong flush on the fast oxidizer, has a mild effect on the mixed or balanced oxidizer, and it has little or no effect on a slow oxidizer.

VITAMIN C TEST: Take 8 grams of vitamin C over an 8-hour period (1,000 milligrams every hour). The fast oxidizer will not feel well, the balanced oxidizer will have a mild response, and the slow oxidizer will have little or no response.

TISSUE MINERAL ANALYSIS: Analysis of mineral status and ratios found in hair can reveal the general rate of metabolic function. I provide this resource at the end of the book.

What kind of food supports the fast oxidizer? These individuals do well with a moderate-protein, high-fat diet to slow down their rate of oxidation and to stabilize their blood sugar. They will also do well on the high-purine foods, such as organ meats, sardines, and anchovies. Their ideal ratio is 35% protein, 15% carbohydrates, and 50% fat. They will benefit from fruits and vegetables more than grains. Slow oxidizers do best with 25% protein, 50% carbohydrates, and 25% fats. They may do best on both plant or animal proteins like chicken, turkey, pork, fish, and eggs. The balanced/mixed oxidizers will burn efficiently using 30% protein, 35% carbohydrates, and 35% fats, as shown in the table below:

Ideal Food Intake Percentages for Each Oxidizer Type			
Type	Protein	Carbohydrates	Fat
Fast oxidizer	35%	15%	50%
Slow oxidizer	25%	50%	25%
Mixed oxidizer	30%	35%	35%

These percentages are not hard-and-fast rules but guide choices. You will know when you feel best, and these ratios can shift due to illness or stress. Experiment with these principles during your dietary changes. Remember that no one does well on refined sugar and refined wheat flour. When one eats well 90% of the time, however, an occasional "refined" food will not be harmful.

Thus, the fast metabolizer is what we would call a carnivore, the slow metabolizer would be on the vegetarian end of the spectrum, and the mixed will benefit from a range of foods. Keep in mind that we are talking about a spectrum.

A plant-based (vegetarian) diet that is rich in plant proteins, fruits, nuts, seeds—and legumes for some—provides a superior foundation for mental health nutrition and will benefit nearly everyone. But not everyone can live on plant proteins alone. Nuts and seeds, especially nut butters, and the grains quinoa and millet are good sources of protein along with well-soaked and well-cooked beans. Depending upon one's individual biochemistry, one can continue as a vegetarian or benefit from adding fish, milk, eggs, and various forms of poultry and meats. The key to a successful plant-based diet is ensuring a diversity of proteins to provide the complement of amino acids necessary for optimal functioning of neurotransmitters in the brain and thus mental health.

TEST FOR AN INCORRECTLY APPLIED VEGETARIAN DIET

People who are depressed, lethargic, anxious, or prone to panic—and who are also following a vegetarian or vegan diet—will improve by including animal proteins into their meals. It is common that such individuals are not aligned with their true dietary needs. Often these individuals are vegetarian for important spiritual, emotional, or environmental reasons; however, genetically their "engines" will not function with vegetarian fuel. If this applies to you and you're willing to try it, I'd suggest an experiment: Try adding animal protein into your diet three times daily for just 7 days, and take notes about any changes you notice in your mood.

SAY NO TO REFINED CARBOHYDRATES AND SUGARS

Mood follows food, and mood swings follow blood sugar swings. Refined carbohydrates, such as sugar and white flour, cause blood sugar to rise sharply and then drop; hence the quick pick-me-up when we grab sugar followed by the just-as-quick letdown within an hour or two as glucose levels drop and fatigue and irritability return.

Thus, the first dietary steps in any movement toward positive, mood-savvy nutritional change are to decrease and eventually to eliminate refined carbohydrates and sugars from your diet, while increasing the intake of quality protein. This is a big step, and many people may at first experience a sort of "withdrawal" from their addiction to refined carbohydrates. But as with any withdrawal, it will pass, and you'll emerge from it feeling better than ever.

A stable mood will for many people remain out of reach until they reduce their intake of refined carbohydrates such as sugar. And some people will never know why they're unable to feel good!

DID YOU KNOW?

Preventing Reactive Hypoglycemia or Maintaining Stable Blood Glucose

The term "hypoglycemia" refers to low blood glucose, which is often associated with poor adrenal function. People under stress are vulnerable to reactive hypoglycemia because stress negatively affects the regulation of blood glucose. Most people who binge on carbohydrates and do not eat a healthy diet have hypoglycemia and do not know it. Many vegetarians experience it, since they often do not consume enough proteins to stabilize their blood sugar. Hypoglycemia contributes to mood swings and inattention. It can easily be mistaken for bipolar disorder or attention-deficit/hyperactivity disorder (ADHD). Children and adults with severe mood swings and irritability commonly experience significant improvement when hypoglycemia and carbohydrate addiction are addressed. People who fall asleep but awaken 3–4 hours later and cannot get back to sleep may also experience nighttime hypoglycemia and will do better eating some protein and carbohydrates just before going to bed.

In general, everyone functions best by eating three to six meals a day, including snacks, and most people would benefit by eliminating refined carbohydrate consumption and combining vegetable and fruit carbohydrates with healthy, high-quality fats like butter, avocado, coconut, nuts, and eggs. Eating organic starchy and nonstarchy vegetables as the primary source of carbohydrates is optimal. Eating small amounts of high-quality protein, fat, and vegetables (with limited fruits) every 3 hours is an essential dietary approach to recovery from hypoglycemia.

FOLLOW THESE GUIDELINES FOR STABLE BLOOD SUGAR

- Eat six small meals a day, or three normal meals with snacks in between.
- Always mix proteins and fats with carbohydrates.
- Consume no refined sugar or flour.

- Eat 2–3 ounces of food every 2–3 hours, depending on need.
- Don't allow yourself to get hungry.
- Never eat carbohydrates alone—always include protein.
- Eat a little before exercise and after.
- Drink plenty of water. Compute half your body weight in lbs., and drink that same number of ounces of water each day (150 lbs. = 75 oz. water daily).

Sample Daily Meal Plan for Glucose Balance		
Time	Snack	Meal
6 a.m.	8 oz. water	1–2 eggs cooked with butter; and some coffee or herbal tea
8 a.m.	2–4 oz. of protein: raw nuts, or (optional) oatmeal with raw butter	
10 a.m.	1 apple (or 1 oz. of dried fruit, such as organic dried apricots), and 10 almonds (or 2 tbsp almond butter)	
12 p.m.		4 oz. of animal protein with 1 sweet potato with butter; and raw vegetables with olive oil and vinegar (or lemon) salad dressing
2 p.m.	1–2 tbsp. nut butter	
4 p.m.	1 hard-boiled egg (or a chocolate—or mocha—smoothie with coconut milk)	
6 p.m.		4–6 oz. protein—either beans or animal protein—with greens—salad and/or steamed, with plenty of olive oil and flax salad dressing and butter (rice noodles or brown rice are optional)
Before bed	2 crackers (gluten-free optional) and 1 oz. of goat cheese; or 1 oz. of turkey or tuna salad	

SAY NO TO INFLAMMATION

One of the most important influences on mental health resulting from poor or nutritionally deficient diet involves the inflammatory response. Inflammation is now understood to underlie depression, cognitive decline, and poor mental health. Reducing inflammation is fundamental to healing, as discussed below.

Common Causes of Inflammation in the Body

- Chronic stress
- Trans fats and refined sugars
- Physical inactivity
- Obesity
- Smoking
- Leaky gut (more on this later)
- Lack of sleep
- Exposure to toxic substances
- Vitamin D deficiency

Everyone is familiar with the inflammation that occurs as a result of an injury, for example when a fall leads to a bruise or cut. The tissue becomes red and swollen, and it is often painful. This is the body's natural immune response, helping us to heal from injuries and infection. Similar inflammation also occurs systemically throughout the body but is often invisible. If this inflammatory response within the body is chronic, cell immune secretions remain turned on all the time. These cells produce proteins called *cytokines* that contribute to depression and to the breakdown of nerve cells.

People who experience major depression have increased levels of inflammatory cytokines that, in turn, negatively affect neurotransmitter function. Certain foods such as refined sugars trigger these inflammatory cytokine responses in the body. These foods are called "dietary stressors." Other foods, like fresh berries, and herbs such as turmeric and ginger, can "quench the fires" of inflammation.

Stress is another cause of inflammation and depression. Relaxation decreases the inflammatory response. The elimination of sugar helps to stabilize mood and reduce systemic inflammation. These are some of the first steps to take in making mood-savvy changes to your diet, whether or not you're experiencing depression or other mood-related health challenges: Reduce stress, eliminate inflammatory foods, and increase the intake of anti-inflammatory foods.

SAY YES TO DIGESTION-SUPPORTING PROBIOTICS

The intestinal tract, or the *gut*, is often called the "second brain" because it is a major source of neurotransmitter production in the body. Thus, it is not surprising that people with chronic digestive problems are often anxious and depressed. Healthy bacteria, known as probiotics, help to lower the stress response by regulating relaxation-related neurotransmitters in the brain. Probiotics may be bought in capsule or liquid form in a health food store and are also found in fermented foods.

Fermented foods are among the best foods for both intestinal and brain health. All traditional diets have some form of fermented foods. The health benefits of yogurt and kefir, among other fermented foods, derive from their beneficial bacteria. The value of fermented foods is well known in traditional cultures everywhere, as they are used to restore and maintain the bowel "garden," where the bacterial flora grow. Yogurt and sauerkraut can be made at home easily and inexpensively and are a wonderful food preparation and "science" experiment to share with children.

Another common practice of our ancestors is making gelatin-rich meat broths that contain collagen and amino acids that are easy to assimilate to help brain function. Freshly made bone and vegetable broth is the first food to choose as a staple in gaining control of your mood and mental wellness. Yet many people no longer cook or prepare foods, relying instead on packages, microwaves, and fast foods. Among the initial steps is to explore how to integrate food preparation, both raw and cooked, into your life.

SAY YES TO GOOD FOOD PREPARATION

Preparing fresh food is an act of self-nourishment, emotionally as well as physically. The stressors of trauma, modern life, and advertising cause us to dissociate from the simple self-care rituals that invigorate us. Many of the suggestions throughout this book are about overcoming the conditioned responses that result from the incessant message that what we put into our bodies doesn't matter to mental health. Food gathering, preparation, and sharing are rituals that, when done well, lead us into a state of relaxation and provide an endorphin rush of attachment and connection. Infusing each step of the nutritional process with a ritual or mindful process enhances relationships as well as digestion and well-being. This social connection is where mental health nutrition begins.

One of the basic themes to consider throughout this book is that good, "real" food is medicine, and "fake" food is toxic to brain health. The second theme is that many foods are psychoactive; that is, they alter consciousness and, like all things that alter consciousness, these foods may be either beneficial or detrimental to mental well-being. Take coffee, for example. Coffee is a drug, not a beverage. Therefore, you should use it as you would a drug—consuming what you need to achieve a desired, beneficial effect without causing negative side effects—and not simply as you would drink a beverage.

SAY YES TO REAL COMFORT FOOD

If your food is not satisfying and at times even comforting, you will not be able to sustain dietary changes.

We often turn to food to relieve stress or unpleasant emotions, which is not inherently a bad thing. The problem arises when we turn to unhealthy, high-carbohydrate, high-sugar, processed foods for comfort. We can use food as part of a self-comforting strategy if we do it with awareness and make choices that will enhance our health rather than put us into a soporific state.

What are comfort foods? Comfort foods are probably different for everybody, but in general they are commonly high-fat, high-sugar, refined carbohydrate foods. The sugars and fats in these foods release opioids in the brain, similar to the way narcotics do, thus creating a pleasure response. Even thinking about these foods can trigger pleasurable brain reactions, just as thinking about juicing a lemon will stimulate salivary flow.

Our definition of comfort food often comes from what our parents gave us as children to calm us down in times of distress, or these foods may be associated with love; they might be sugary foods like donuts, cookies, and refined carbohydrates. White foods in general seem to be common comfort foods—such as potatoes, bread, sour cream, bananas, and sugar. Comfort food may provide a nostalgic feeling related to cultural or familial traditions. Often we are drawn to comfort food when we haven't had a chance to prepare healthy foods.

TRY THIS!

Awareness While Eating: Chewing the Raisin

How might you prepare in advance to preempt the need for comfort food but still satisfy and nourish yourself?

Sometimes we seek comfort in food when what we really need is to nourish ourselves with the moment-to-moment attention called mindfulness. Use this mindfulness exercise with a raisin to obtain self-awareness about food, as well as relief from stress:

Hold a raisin and observe it as though you are the first person to ever touch a raisin and you are investigating for the first time. See the raisin in all of its detail; observe every part of it—the wrinkles, the way the light shines on it, and so on. Touch the raisin and explore the texture and sensation. Smell the raisin and inhale its aroma; take note of how this fragrance may stimulate your stomach or mouth. Gently and slowly place the raisin in your mouth and, before chewing, take time to notice how it feels on your tongue and any other sensations you notice. Prepare to chew the raisin by slowly finding out how to position it for chewing. Chew the raisin a couple of times and notice what happens when you do, really tasting it in all of its subtle complexities. Before swallowing, notice how the texture of the raisin changes as you chew it. When you are ready, think about swallowing the raisin and experience the intention of swallowing. Then swallow the raisin. Afterward, see if you can feel the raisin as it moves to your stomach. Observe how you feel after this exercise in relaxation and mindful eating.

We crave foods for a variety of reasons: We need the nutrients they offer, and the body provides a message to eat those foods. People often remark that they get a craving for beef, for example. We also crave foods that we are allergic to; these foods function like a drug. Gluten-containing foods can trigger opiod-like reactions and gluten bingeing is a sign of this reactivity. We crave food that reminds us of a certain time in our life, linked to people we have loved and lost, or comfort foods that are linked to our country of origin or holiday times. We also crave foods to alter consciousness, such as for comfort and anxiety reduction (carbohydrates and fats), or for energy and focus (proteins and dopamine-rich coffee). Foods we crave provide chemical reactions that the brain/mind wants and needs. The key is to become familiar with our unique "craving" profile—to learn which foods we crave and when we crave them, to understand the (emotional) biochemistry of the foods, and to find substitutions that address these needs but are healthier and without the side effects. This is the "principle of substitutions," which means finding an alternative food to provide the same effect, substituting a healthy food or substance for a less healthy one.

Comfort food examples may include grilled cheese sandwiches, mashed potatoes, pancakes, bread, pizza, macaroni and cheese, frozen lasagna, spaghetti and meatballs, Danish pastry, coffee cake, fried chicken, fast food in general, pie, donuts, Chinese food, egg rolls, frosting, and chocolate. Each culture also has its own specific comfort foods—for example, in Great Britain these include fish and chips, custard, pies, puddings, soups and stews, bangers and mash; there is *pierogi* from Poland; *kvass* and borscht from Russia; and baked beans, meatloaf, macaroni and cheese, fish sticks, pot pies, and chicken noodle soup in the United States. Many of these foods can still be part of a healthy "comfort" self-soothing plan when you change some of the ingredients. For example, make mashed potato (or mashed sweet potato) with ghee and sea salt; baked sweet potato fries dipped in homemade mayonnaise; gluten-free macaroni and cheese; homemade pizza with gluten-free crust and homemade sauce, topped with vegetables and organic sausage; healthy homemade almond-chocolate treats; and coconut black rice pudding.

Healthy Substitutes for Unhealthy Comfort Foods	
Unhealthy comfort foods	Healthy substitutions
Sugary breads or sweets	Sweet potatoes and raw butter
Sugary treats	Smoothie with fat, sweetened with stevia
Chocolate with sugar	Unsweetened cocoa powder with stevia (or homemade stevia-sweetened chocolate candy)
Cane sugar	Honey or maple syrup
Honey	Stevia
Coffee	Black tea, decaffeinated coffee, herbal coffee substitutes (roasted dandelion root, ramón nut [breadnut]), green tea, chai

NEXT STEPS

- Balance mood by stabilizing blood glucose levels.
- Eat breakfast, lunch, dinner, and a snack before sleep.
- Decrease stimulant foods if anxious.
- Reduce or eliminate sugar/refined foods.
- Eliminate "enriched" foods.
- Identify comfort foods.
- Plan healthy nutritional "substitutions."
- Identify the changes you want to make, focusing first on what will help you feel successful.

CHAPTER 4

Digestion FAQ:
Get Smart About the
Second Brain

The brain inside our skull is what I like to call the "first brain." It's like our personal air traffic control, overseeing and orchestrating all the major traffic in the body and mind. Our gut, which is also called the "second brain," communicates with the first brain via a complex system similar to a highway with overpasses, bridges, exits, and stop and go lights. It controls the digestive system via a network of over 100 million nerves and chemicals that send messages to the central nervous system, and this "brain" allows us to think and feel in a way that comes from the "gut." You're probably familiar with the idea of gut wisdom. When we say, "I just feel in my gut that is right," or "my gut is telling me no," that sensation is the second brain communicating with the first. For example, the feeling of "butterflies in the stomach" describes one way we experience stress in the gut. Feeling and sensation are part of the gut's function, and it is deeply linked to our emotional lives and intuition. It is also a crucial factor in our mental health and wellbeing.

The following is a list of key questions that are related to digestion and the second brain:

Q: WHY SHOULDN'T WE EAT WHEN WE'RE STRESSED?

A: Stress is the enemy of digestion, and poor digestion blocks us from absorbing crucial nutrients from the things we eat.

The second brain controls the breakdown and absorption of foods, elimination of waste, and the bowel rhythms that move food toward elimination.

In order to digest, we must be relaxed. Stress can slow down or stop the digestive process. When the nervous system goes into a "fight, flight, or freeze" response, it impairs digestive muscle contractions, reduces the secretion of digestive enzymes, and redirects blood flow away from the digestive organs where it is needed for digestion and instead floods the extremities and muscles with blood, which are now poised for an emergency response.

Stress wreaks havoc on the digestive system, causing diaphragm spasms (hiccups), a rise in stomach acid (heartburn), nausea, diarrhea, and/or constipation. It exacerbates digestive disorders like inflammatory bowel disease, stomach ulcers, and celiac disease.

TRY THIS!

Mindful Eating

Try this mindfulness exercise to prepare for a relaxed digestive experience.

Observe yourself chewing. Pay attention to the texture and flavors of the food, the smells, and the position of the food on the plate. Embrace the whole of the sensory experience. The production of saliva breaks down the food and tends to enhance the experience of texture and flavors on different parts of the tongue. Chew every bite until it is liquid in the mouth, allowing the food to travel down the throat and into the belly.

Stress impairs digestion, and poor digestion affects the neurochemicals that influence mood and well-being. Like the first brain, the second brain uses over 30 neurotransmitters; a whopping 95% of the serotonin in the body—which improves mood and the ability to digest carbohydrates—is produced in the gut.

Impaired digestion of protein means the amino acids are not available to the brain to support neurotransmitter production, directly affecting mood, sleep, and cravings. The overuse of antibiotics, along with insufficient prebiotics in the diet to prepare the garden of the intestines to grow healthy gut microbiota, impairs the production of neurotransmitters and subsequently causes mood problems like depression and anxiety.

TRY THIS!

The Power Lunch

The "power lunch" refers to eating a lunch of protein, fat, and vegetables (no grains or alcohol) when negotiating an important communication such as a contract or job interview and gaining a mental edge by staying alert and awake without the sedating effects of grains and starchy carbohydrates.

Simple Steps to Relax Your Digestion

- Eat in places that induce relaxation rather than places where you feel stressed.
- Employ rituals such as communal eating, giving thanks, and potlucks; this can also reduce stress and improve digestion.
- Breathe slowly and rhythmically before eating and during the meal.
- Eat with others when possible and without the distraction of a TV or computer.
- Put your fork or spoon down between bites and let it sit for 15–30 seconds or more.
- Chew food 50 times or until almost liquid.
- Set out nutrients on a table in the kitchen organized by whether they are to be taken before the meal, during the meal, or after the meal.
- Set a goal to reduce or eliminate smoking, caffeine, and alcohol consumption, all of which impair digestion and are major stress factors.

Q: HOW DOES FOOD INFLUENCE EMOTIONAL BALANCE?

A: Stability is all about choosing the right nutritional building blocks.

Would you feel safe in a house constructed of pick-up sticks? They might last for a while, but the first big wind or rain (stressor) would blow it all down. Our body and mind are the same. We can survive for a while on poor quality foods, but they won't nourish the brain for the hard stressors and coping that modern life requires.

Food is made up of carbohydrates, proteins, fats, water, vitamins, and minerals. Carbohydrates are sugars, starches, and fibers—either simple (as in fruits, vegetables, and sugars) or complex (as in whole grains, starchy vegetables, and beans). The purpose of digestion is to break down these foods into smaller particles so they can be absorbed into the bloodstream and used throughout the body. Digestion releases the nutrients in food so that the body can utilize them. This process takes place in the gastrointestinal tract. Carbohydrates break down into glucose, which supports brain function. Proteins—from meat, beans, eggs, and dairy products—are broken down into smaller molecules called amino acids, which are the building blocks of neurotransmitters that also support brain function.

Good Fats and Fats to Avoid

Fats provide energy and lubrication for the brain and insulation for body organs and the body generally. Introducing good-quality fats into the diet as both foods and supplements and eliminating poor-quality fats is an important first step to begin a nutritional program of recovery. Fats are essential for the absorption of nutrients, particularly the fat-soluble vitamins A, D, E, and K. These vitamins require fat to enable them to be transported to cells. Low-fat diets, for example, may adversely affect mental health due to inadequate levels of these essential vitamins. It is a medical myth that saturated fats are dangerous. Saturated animal fats (from pasture-fed livestock and some wild seafoods) provide fat-soluble vitamins A, D, and K_2. A complement of fats from animals, vegetables, nuts, and seeds extracted via a "cold process" should be integrated with all other oils into a daily diet—along with eggs, which are rich in choline to support the brain and memory.

Changing your diet to include healthy fats for brain function is one positive behavior that is easy to accomplish. The second behavior you need to do is to eliminate the use of unhealthy fats or trans-fatty acids.

Most commercially processed foods—such as cookies, margarine, shortening, crackers, chips, salad dressings, and snack foods—contain trans-fatty acids from ingredients such as "partially hydrogenated" oils as well as deodorized vegetable oils, all of which are dangerous for mental well-being.

The following table lists the beneficial fats and the fats that you should avoid when possible:

Good fats	Fats to avoid
Traditional fats such as butter, coconut oil, tallow, and suet (from cows and lambs); fat from ducks, geese, chickens, and turkey; and lard from pigs are all "saturated" fats. A variety of fish oils from krill, sardines, salmon, and cod can easily be integrated into the diet. Olive oil, full-fat dairy products, and red meat from lamb, beef, and wildlife—such as deer, elk, moose, and bear. Nuts, seeds, fish, and leafy greens also contain polyunsaturated fats.	A commercially created form of fat that does not occur in nature is called "trans fat." Trans fats are a contaminant by-product of commercial hydrogenation of vegetable oils. Preparing foods with hydrogenated oils may result in food containing high levels of trans fats.

This table lists the beneficial fats and their health benefits:

Good fat	Health benefits
Raw butter	Ideal balance of Omega-3 and Omega-6 fatty acids Provides vitamins A, D, and E; iodine; lecithin; and selenium Provides trace minerals such as chromium, copper, manganese, and zinc Supports immune function Increases metabolism Protects against pathogens in the intestinal tract Supports thyroid health Supports brain function and prostaglandin balance Assists with the absorption of fat-soluble vitamins A, E, and K
Poultry fat (chicken, duck, and goose)	High in vitamin E High in Omega-3 and Omega-6 Supports brain function Prevents cognitive decline
Coconut oil	Anti-inflammatory Antibacterial Antifungal Antiviral Antioxidant Lowers blood sugar Protects the liver Improves immune function

Clarified butter (ghee)	Helps to heal gastrointestinal inflammations Contains butyric acid, which has antiviral and anticancer properties May help prevent dementia Promotes digestion and assimilation Provides benefits of butter without the proteins that cause allergies
Palm and palm-kernel oil	Provides lycopene Provides pro-vitamin A carotenes Rich in vitamins E, K, and CoQ_{10} Improves cholesterol levels Supports healthy blood pressure levels Anti-inflammatory Supports healthy brain function, protecting against neurological disorders
Cold-pressed extra-virgin olive oil	Anti-inflammatory Provides antioxidants such as vitamin E and beta-carotene Reduces blood pressure Slows the growth of unwanted bacteria in the digestive tract Improves cognitive function, including visual memory Improves brain and nervous system function
Avocado oil	Anti-inflammatory Provides carotenoid antioxidants Provides vitamins C and E Provides manganese, selenium, and zinc Rich in Omega-3 fatty acids Helps regulate blood sugar
Cold-pressed sesame oil	Provides antioxidants Lowers blood pressure Reduces sodium in the blood Reduces blood sugar Antidepressant
Eggs	Rich in choline, an anti-inflammatory nutrient for the brain and memory Provide calcium, iron, phosphorus, zinc, thiamine, vitamin B6, folate, pantothenic acid, and vitamin B_{12} Provide the fat-soluble vitamins A, D, and E Provide Omega-3 fatty acids Provide lutein and zeaxanthin for better eye health Contain a cholesterol that is a precursor for production of hormones in the body, including the sex hormones testosterone and estrogen Contain a cholesterol that does not raise blood cholesterol
Lard (from pigs)	Excellent source of vitamin D Lowers LDL cholesterol

Tallow (from beef and lamb)	Good source of antimicrobial palmitoleic acid
Walnut oil	Use only raw, and not for cooking Rich in Omega-3 fatty acids Reduces inflammation Supports healthy hormone levels Provides selenium, phosphorus, iron, magnesium, calcium, and zinc Contains antioxidants
Cold-pressed flax oil (use uncooked only)	Good source of Omega-3 fatty acids Supplies nutrient-rich lignans Supports healthy cholesterol levels Supports blood glucose levels Rich in alpha-linolenic acid (ALA)
Pumpkin seed oil	Anti-inflammatory Provides tryptophan Increases good cholesterol Reduces blood pressure
Grapeseed oil (high cooking temperature)	Can be heated up to 485 degrees F, making it a good cooking oil Rich in linoleic acid Provides polyphenols (flavonoids) Provides vitamin E Anti-inflammatory Antioxidant Antihistamine Adaptogenic (anti-stress)

Carbohydrates

Sugar is the simplest form of carbohydrate and is found in fruit, vegetables, dairy products, and refined sugar itself. Complex carbohydrates are either starch or fiber. Starchy vegetables—such as carrots, potatoes, and peas—and grains—such as wheat, rice, barley, and oats—are sources of starch. Starches can also be from refined foods, such as cornstarch, chips, and certain dessert foods. Complex carbohydrates provide energy and fiber in the diet.

Proteins

Proteins are the third category of nutrients essential to both mental and physical health. They fuel every function of living cells. Proteins are derived from either animal or plant sources, and they must be broken down by digestion into amino acids in order to be used by the body. Animal proteins such as whey, eggs, beef, casein, and fish differ from plant proteins such as soy, pea, hemp, and rice in many ways, including cholesterol and saturated fat levels, digestion rates, allergens, and their amino acid profiles.

Everyone has a different level of need for protein; some need more protein than others (remember the table in Chapter 3 where we looked at different protein, fat and carbohydrate needs in different populations). However, during times of stress, or intense physical exertion, proteins are more essential for everyone; they support growth and repair in the body, which tends to break down under stress.

HOW TO CALCULATE YOUR PROTEIN NEED

You will want to adjust these calculations to whether you are a fast, slow, or mixed oxidizer. Remember, a fast oxidizer is a natural carnivore and will use animal protein and fats more efficiently than a slow oxidizer, so experiment with these numbers. Remember to pay attention to how you feel.

For general health maintenance, take 50% of your body weight in grams. A 150-pound individual might consume about 75 grams of protein divided into 4–6 meals during the day.

> For a short-term intensive muscle-building or fat-loss program, take .75–1 gram of protein per pound of bodyweight. A 150-pound individual would consume 75–100 grams of protein during a day.

Protein requirements increase if you are doing vigorous exercise or if you are trying to build muscle and lose fat. It is especially important for elder individuals to build muscle mass through exercise and to consume enough protein to support this muscle mass. People who eat the standard American diet tend to over-consume poor-quality protein at nearly twice the amount that is necessary, while vegetarians tend to under-consume proteins. Both approaches can harm mental health. Protein from animal foods have higher amounts and proportions of the essential amino acids. Another challenge in vegetarian diets is the failure to consistently combine proteins that have complete amino acids, and this can lead to deficits in neurotransmitter synthesis.

The following table lists beneficial proteins and the proteins you should try to avoid:

Good proteins	Proteins to avoid
Organic, free-range, minimally processed, humanely raised meats	Soy, soy protein isolates, commercially processed animal products
Pastured eggs from a local farmer	Commercially raised eggs or animal products with hormones and antibiotics

Eggs are a perfect protein and provide about 5 grams of protein per egg, the equivalent of a handful of nuts or seeds. Milk and yogurt provide about 10 grams of protein per cup (milk products are best eaten raw and unpasteurized). Beans, cottage cheese, and tofu each provide about 15 grams of protein per cup. Meat, chicken, and fish provide about 25 grams of protein per 3- to 4-ounce serving.

Proteins and Feeling Full

Proteins, along with vegetables, are part of the satiety complex. Proteins such as nuts, seeds, and whey, along with greens, cruciferous vegetables, and root vegetables, all give the sensation of being full and satisfied. This is a helpful sensation to have when you are making dietary changes or if you have hypoglycemia, compulsive and night eating syndrome, or bulimia. Eating 10 raw almonds is ideal as a snack or at the start of a meal. I can think of no simpler daily habit that supports brain health and a relaxed mood.

Protein deficiency may occur in people on a strict vegetarian diet who do not consume adequate amounts of plant proteins, or who do not combine them so they get the complement of all amino acids. Bulimia, fruitarian diets, diets high in refined carbohydrates, and alcoholic liver damage also contribute to protein insufficiency, which in turn affects amino acid and neurotransmitter levels. Symptoms of protein deficiency include a lack of mental focus, emotional instability, impaired immune function, fatigue, hair loss, and slow wound healing.

Q: DOES DIGESTION START WHEN FOOD REACHES THE GUT?

A: No. Digestion begins with how food is prepared. Chewing is also an essential part of digestion.
Digestion of food begins with how it is prepared. Cooked foods are more easily digested than raw foods. Fuel in the form of food goes into the mouth and begins the process of digestion with the mechanical movement of chewing and the secretion of saliva, which breaks down starches.

Under stress, we eat too rapidly and swallow food whole—the acids and enzymes required to break down food cannot then do their job. With food undigested in the belly, pains and gases develop, perhaps medications are used to quell the discomfort, nutrients are malabsorbed, and organs including the brain are malnourished. Eating food slowly, however, involves chewing our food into smaller particles so it can be digested, and it allows for the initial breakdown of starches.

Stress can also affect digestion at the esophageal sphincter, which—like a drawbridge—may open when it is supposed to close or close when it is supposed to open. Sometimes it relaxes too much and closes on part of the stomach, pushing the stomach up, which is called a hiatal hernia. When the sphincter does not close effectively, this allows stomach acid to rise into the lower esophagus, causing acid reflux, or gastroesophageal reflux disease (GERD).

TRY THIS!

Adrenal Support Tea

This tea is made with four herbal ingredients, and is a delicious Ayurvedic medicine recipe that is designed to support the adrenal glands, aid digestion, enhance energy, and reduce allergic reactions. **Licorice root** is soothing to mucous membranes and reduces stress and fatigue. **Fennel seed** reduces gas and aids digestion. **Fenugreek seed** is very soothing to the intestines and is a natural antihistamine. **Peppermint leaf** reduces intestinal gas and **flax seed** also aids and soothes the alimentary tract. The recommended dosage is 1 cup per day. Note that too much licorice can raise blood pressure by causing fluid retention, so don't overdo it.

A good herbal or natural foods store will have the following ingredients:

Ingredients

1 oz. licorice root (pieces)

1 oz. fennel seed

1 oz. fenugreek seed

2 oz. flax seed

1 oz. peppermint leaf

Directions

1. Mix all the ingredients together while dry and store in a glass jar in a dark cabinet.
2. Take 1 heaping teaspoon of the mixture and simmer in 2 cups of water for 15 minutes.
3. Strain and drink hot or cold in the morning or midday.

Steps to Address Acid Reflux and GERD

1. Apply an ice pack to the ribs at the xiphoid process (where the diaphragm is) for 15 minutes before eating. (GERD often co-occurs with chronic stress, PTSD, or with a hiatal hernia.)
2. Take the following nutrients to prevent and reduce GERD:
   - Chlorophyll and vitamin U (Gastrazyme™)
   - Zinc carnosine
   - Digestive enzymes
   - 1 oz. fresh cabbage juice (alternative to Gastrazyme)
3. Follow these dietary guidelines:

- Don't eat refined or starchy carbohydrates (breads, pastas, rice, etc. during an acute episode).
- Eliminate coffee. If you must, drink cold brew coffee only.
- Avoid eating citrus fruits, tomatoes, and spicy foods.
- Relax and rest.

Q: WHAT PARTS OF THE BODY'S DIGESTIVE SYSTEM INFLUENCE MOOD, AND IN WHAT WAYS?

A: Each organ in the digestive system works both independently and together with others to form the mood-influencing functions of the second brain.
Below, I describe some of the main players in this process, with brief overviews of how each of them functions as a key component in mood-savvy digestion.

The Gallbladder and Liver

The liver produces bile, a greenish substance rich in bile salts, and the gallbladder supports liver function by storing and concentrating the bile which is then released when food arrives to the upper intestine. The bile salts emulsify the fats needed to elevate mood and decrease stress as well as to maintain artery health and reduce inflammation. Normally, the liver and gallbladder work together to break down fats, just like dish soap breaks down the grease in a frying pan. If the gallbladder is not functioning well, these fats will not be as effectively emulsified and fats be less effective in reaching the brain where they are needed for mental well-being.

Contrary to the conventional belief that a person with gallbladder problems must follow a low-fat diet, a very low-fat diet can cause the gallbladder's "muscle motor" to slow down. This special muscle pushes out bile into the duodenum. When the muscle fails, it leads to a buildup of sludge, like a stagnant pond that backs up. Removing the gallbladder is like throwing out the garbage pail because it's full. Just empty it out and clean it. Good-quality oils—in particular a regular dose of olive oil mixed with lemon juice—help to move this "sludge" along and can prevent gall bladder disease.

Junk food, refined foods, trans-fatty acids, and excessive alcohol contribute to chronic gallbladder congestion, low bile output, gravel, and gallstones. Other symptoms of gallbladder problems include burping, flatulence, a feeling of heaviness after a meal, shoulder pain, pain under the ribs on the right side or in the back directly behind the diaphragm, and nausea. Awakening with bloodshot eyes after a heavy meal the night before is another sign of gallbladder distress.

If you have had your gallbladder removed, replacement supplements should include natural ox bile, betaine, taurine, vitamin C, and pancreatic enzyme supplements that include lipase. These nutrients will support fat digestion. (See the Resources section for a product called "Beta Plus.")

TRY THIS!

Gall Bladder Beet Recipe

Beets and beet tops are rich in betaine, and along with virgin olive oil and lemon are about the best combination of foods for a healthy gallbladder, which leads to good mental health. Steamed beets and beet greens are easy to prepare.

1. Cut the beet greens off at the root and wash and put aside for later use. Scrub the beets gently and place them in a steamer basket with their skins intact. They will take about an hour to cook. Avoid piercing them because the juices and nutrients will come out.
2. When they are done steaming and have cooled off enough to handle, remove the skin by running them under cool water and rubbing them.
3. Dice or slice, and drench in olive oil and fresh lemon juice. Serve warm or cold.
4. Chop ¼ of a medium onion; add to a pan along with 1 crushed clove of garlic. Take the well-cleaned, chopped beet greens and add to the pan. Stir, and sautée over low heat until just soft. And a touch of tamari, a sprinkle of cayenne pepper, and serve.

Options: Set some aside before adding olive oil and lemon and use the next day in a vegetable smoothie, or top with goat yogurt and a dash of dill.

The Pancreas

The pancreas is a glandular organ that secretes proteolytic (protein-digesting) enzymes that help to further break down starches, fats, and proteins. The pancreas secretes digestive enzymes into the small intestine that help to break down the gastric juices and partly digested food that has just left the stomach and entered the duodenum. Pancreatic enzymes, including supplemental proteolytic enzymes, improve mental health by reducing inflammation.

DIGESTIVE ENZYMES REDUCE INFLAMMATION AND PAIN

Try this! Green Papaya Salad

Proteolytic enzymes digest protein. They serve two vital health functions:

1. When taken with food, these inexpensive enzymes help to digest food protein and help to reduce food allergies.
2. When taken on an empty stomach, they "digest" inflammatory cells/proteins and improve immune function, reduce pain, inhibit the formation of fibrin in damaged tissues, and increase circulation to inflamed areas.

Food and supplement sources for these anti-inflammatories are papain (from green papaya), bromelain (from unripe pineapple), and serratiopeptidase (from the silkworm). Food sources of proteolytic enzymes include fresh pineapple and green papaya.

Ingredients

1 large clove garlic, peeled

¼ tsp. coarse sea salt

2 tbsp. dry-roasted peanuts

1 serrano chili pepper, thinly sliced

1 tbsp. fresh cilantro stems (save the leaves for topping)

1 tbsp. minced, peeled, fresh ginger

2 tbsp. fresh lime juice

1 tbsp. fish sauce

1 medium, green (unripe) papaya

5 drops stevia (optional)

lettuce for serving

grilled beef, or fresh steamed shrimp, or chicken (optional)

Directions

1. Coarsely blend the garlic, salt, peanuts, chilies, cilantro, ginger, and stevia into a thick sauce.
2. Place in a large bowl and add fresh lime juice and fish sauce (tamari can substitute for vegetarian diets).

3. Cut the papaya in half lengthwise, scrape and toss the seeds, and then slice the fruit (julienne) into long thin strips.

4. Add the papaya to a mixing bowl and toss so the sauce is well distributed. Taste and adjust the seasoning as needed.

5. Place lettuce leaves on a platter and then the papaya salad. Top with cold jumbo shrimp, sliced beef, or cold steamed sliced chicken. Sprinkle with peanuts and cilantro leaves and serve cold.

Note: Green papaya can be found at local Asian or Mexican/Central American groceries.

The Intestines

What makes your garden grow? The intestines are like a garden; indeed, the whole digestive tract has come to be known as the *microbiome*. Think of it like your neighborhood community with people of all kinds. Like your neighborhood, your microbiome is a community of a variety of microorganisms, some friendly and others not. A healthy neighborhood predominates with friendly people who cooperate and support each other and effectively manage the troublemakers. So it is with a healthy microbiome: It can tolerate some dissension but too much leads to illness that, if not addressed, can be damaging to the whole neighborhood (digestive system) and then affect the surrounding communities (such as the brain, which relates to mental health).

This microbiome is where the "gut-brain" connection plays on its seesaws, communicating back and forth, feeding the neighborhood, including the first brain. Healthy intestinal bacteria populate the microbiome "garden" and when in abundance keep levels of unhealthy bacteria from overpopulating. When there are healthy bacteria, the anti-anxiety neurotransmitters like GABA are produced and keep anxiety low.

One of our goals with nutrition is to support the healthy members of the microbiome community so the dangerous ones will go elsewhere.

Leaky Gut

The intestines are a gatekeeper—they keep toxins and proteins out of the bloodstream that do not belong and they allow nutrients that do. Think of the drain in the kitchen sink. The finer the mesh, the more waste it collects, and the less problematic waste goes down the drain. The larger the mesh, the more particles get through and cause problems because they should not have breached the drain. Hence, the concept of "leaky gut" or intestinal permeability refers to when toxins and allergens breach this intestinal barrier.

These toxins then travel to the brain. Symptoms of leaky gut or permeability include abdominal pain, food allergies and intolerances, cognitive and memory problems, and the risk of alcoholism, autism, ADHD, and multiple food and chemical sensitivities.

The following nutrients support recovery from leaky gut:
- Glutamine
- Turmeric

TRY THIS!

Slippery Elm Bark Tea for Intestinal Health and Leaky Gut Support
Slippery elm bark is mucilaginous and soothing to the mucous membranes. It's good for GERD as well as leaky gut. Obtain slippery elm bark powder and add a teaspoon of powder to 2 cups of water, then bring to a boil. Reduce the heat and gently simmer for 15–20 minutes, then strain. It will be almost pudding-like, and that's fine. Add a touch of cinnamon for taste, and drink it or use a spoon. (Caution: Slippery elm bark is not for use during pregnancy or nursing.)

Large Intestine, Rectum, and Anus

Once nutrients are absorbed through the walls of the small intestine into the bloodstream, what is left is undigested food. This becomes a waste product that moves into the large intestine (colon), where any remaining water and nutrients are absorbed. As water is extracted, the waste becomes solid in the form of stool, which then passes toward the rectum, which holds the stool until it is pushed out through the anus.

Stress and nutritionally related digestive problems can also affect this final end of the alimentary canal—at the rectum and anus. For example, if fecal matter does not have enough fluid or fiber, it can lead to constipation and hemorrhoids.

TRY THIS!

A Special Recipe to Treat Hemorrhoids

I learned about this remedy from the immunologist Dr. Nicholas Gonzalez. Take a ripe banana and peel it. Lay the peels, inner skin side up, on a sheet of wax paper. With a spoon, gently scrape the inner pulp away from the skin and place it on the wax paper. Toss the leftover skins and now shape the pulp into round pellets small enough to fit into the anus. Once they are formed, place them one by one on the wax paper and transfer the paper to a cookie sheet and place in the freezer. When they are frozen take 1 or 2 of these pellets and before bed insert them gently just into the anal opening. The pulp is rich in vitamin C and bioflavonoids, which will reduce the inflammation and help the swelling heal.

The polarity tea and slipper elm bark mentioned above are also helpful for hemorrhoids.

Q: SHOULD I ELIMINATE CHOLESTEROL FROM MY DIET?

A: No. Cholesterol is necessary for proper brain and nervous system function.

Cholesterol is frequently condemned as a major cause of heart disease, but this is untrue. Cholesterol is necessary for proper brain and nervous system function, and it is an important part of our ability to use serotonin, thereby preventing depression. Cholesterol is also essential to produce vitamin D. Low levels of vitamin D are associated with chronic pain and depression. Low levels of cholesterol are associated with autism, including anxiety, muscle pain, and suicide attempts. People have differing needs for cholesterol; some do well with total cholesterol at 240 and others do well at 180. For those whose cholesterol dips too low for their individual needs, anxiety may follow. Bottom line, do not be afraid of cholesterol and do not artificially force it to a lower level in your body.

Q: WHAT MAKES FIBER SO GOOD FOR DIGESTIVE HEALTH?

A: Intake of digestible fiber is essential to a healthy colon and a clean engine.

There are digestible and nondigestible forms of fiber. The fiber sources that are indigestible carbohydrates are found in natural plant foods such as leafy green vegetables, fruits, legumes, nuts, and grains. Fiber has no calories or food energy, and yet it is a crucial component of a healthy diet. It passes through the digestive tract undigested, but in the process it sweeps up the debris along the colon walls and adds content to the digested food. Each day, women and men should obtain at least 25 grams and 38 grams of fiber, respectively. Fiber also signals to stop eating, which then suppresses the appetite.

There are two types of fiber: soluble and insoluble. Many seeds and plants provide both types of fiber

Soluble fiber	Insoluble fiber
Chia seeds, oat bran, nuts, beans, lentils, psyllium husk, peas, barley, and some fruits and vegetables	Wheat bran, corn, whole grains, oat bran, seeds and nuts, brown rice, flaxseed, and the skins of many fruits and vegetables

Soluble fiber slows down digestion by absorbing water and forming a gel in the digestive tract. It increases the feeling of fullness, and it slows down the rate at which the stomach empties, which also slows down the absorption of glucose, making it essential in the diets of people with diabetes. Insoluble fiber does not dissolve in water but rather absorbs water and puffs up like a sponge, passing through the digestive tract and helping to push materials through. In this way it helps prevent constipation, providing a laxative effect.

FIBER FLUSH

Take 1 teaspoon of psyllium husk and mix with 8 ounces of water. Drink this mixture, followed by another 8 ounces of water. Do this one hour before your meal, 3 times a day for 3 days. This will contribute to flushing the colon of waste.

Q: WHAT ARE "PREBIOTICS" AND "PROBIOTICS," WHY DO THEY MATTER, AND HOW DO I BOOST THEM?

A: Prebiotics and probiotics are healthy foods and microorganisms that promote proper digestive functioning and protect the body from harmful bacteria.

Prebiotics

Prebiotics set the stage in the colonic "garden" so probiotics or microbiota can flourish and not allow the harmful bacteria to propagate, much like healthy soil allows seeds to develop into fruit and be resistant to the effects of "pests." Prebiotics are soluble indigestible dietary fibers that support the beneficial gut microbiota (bacteria) that live in the colon.

Foods containing prebiotics include:
- Raw and cooked onions
- Garlic
- Jerusalem artichokes
- Leeks
- Asparagus
- Wheat
- Beans
- Bananas
- Agave
- Dandelion
- Chicory root
- Chia

TRY THIS!

Prebiotic-Infused Water

Soak a tablespoon of chia or flax seeds in 8 ounces of water every evening and place covered in the fridge. In the morning drink it upon awakening. It will serve as an effective prebiotic, satiety drink and provide fatty acids and fiber for intestinal health.

Probiotics

Probiotics are beneficial live microorganisms that colonize the intestines, maintaining a balance of the beneficial gut bacteria. There are 400–500 different kinds of healthy bacteria in the gut. They prevent infections, diarrhea, and inflammation, and they improve immune health. They also produce nutrients, such as vitamin K and the B vitamins. Probiotics are also called "psychobiotics," because they improve mood and have been shown to reduce anxiety and stress.

Probiotics include fermented foods, such as the following:
- Sauerkraut
- Pickles
- Kombucha
- Kimchi
- Miso
- Micro-algaes
- Brewer's yeast
- Yogurt and cheeses with live cultures

It is best to avoid emulsifiers. These are products like carboxymethylcellulose and polysorbate-80 that are added to packaged foods and are listed on labels. They alter the probiotic garden, thus causing inflammation, and they contribute to obesity.

TRY THIS!

Spices and Herbs to Enhance Digestion and Reduce "Gas"
Fennel and licorice are often used after an Indian meal to reduce gas, just like the Mexican culinary tradition of adding the herbs cumin and epazote (Dysphania ambrosioides), also known as wormseed, to cooked beans to enrich flavor and aid digestion. Add black pepper, dill, basil, ginger, cardamom, and parsley to cooked or raw food to reduce gas, and drink a cup of peppermint tea following a meal.

Q: WHAT'S ONE SIMPLE WAY I CAN ADAPT MY EATING HABITS TO ENHANCE DIGESTION?

A: Learn to eat smart food combinations! Some food combinations complement each other's requirements for digestion, whereas other combinations compete with each other for digestive juices and enzymes, thus leading to indigestion.

Food Combinations

If you are taking digestive enzymes and eating well, but you still have digestive trouble, it is worth looking into simplifying how you are combining foods. Eating only one or two types of food that combine well together (foods that require similar acid-based or alkaline-based enzymes) enhances digestion. Combining large amounts of starch, like noodles, with protein foods like meat, for example, is likely to result in feeling digestive upset. Certain food combinations will not digest well because of the way digestion works.

One way to think about food combining is to consider the mixing or combining of various paint colors; while you might mix any compatible colors together, if you mix several competing colors at once the results become muddied. While some colors work well together and enhance the overall palette, others do not. Food combining works in a similar way. Starches are digested in the mouth with the enzymes present in saliva, whereas protein is digested by stomach acid. If you ask the body to simultaneously produce both an acid environment (to digest protein) alongside alkalinizing enzymes in order to digest starches, it can delay digestion as the body figures out which food takes priority. This often leads to fermentation and gas.

Five Rules of Smart Food Combination
1. Eat fruit separately from meals by at least 30 minutes—longer if eating the fruit after a meal.
2. Drink water and other liquids, especially cold liquids, at least 30–60 minutes before a meal but not with the meal.
3. Avoid combining proteins with starchy vegetables and grains.
4. Combine nonstarchy vegetables with animal proteins.
5. Combine nonstarchy vegetables and fats with starches like grains, seeds, and starchy vegetables.

To help you follow these rules of food combination, here is a list of which foods fall into the various categories:

- **Nonstarchy vegetables include** leafy greens, broccoli, asparagus, cauliflower, carrots, bok choy, cabbage, celery, lettuce, green beans, garlic, fennel, onions, chives, turnips, sprouts, red radish, yellow squash, zucchini, cucumber, and beets. Nonstarchy vegetables and ocean vegetables can be combined with proteins, oils and butter, grains, starchy vegetables, lemons and limes, and soaked and sprouted nuts and seeds.
- **Starchy vegetables include** acorn and butternut squash, lima beans, peas, corn, water chestnuts, artichokes, pumpkin, and potatoes.
- **Starches include** cereals and grains, dried beans, pasta, breads, and peas.
- **Fats and oils combine with** vegetables, grains, and protein. Avoid large amounts of fat with protein (like the mayonnaise in tuna salad) because it slows digestion. Instead, use a small amount of oil to cook, and use oil-free dressings.
- **Protein fats include** avocado, olives, seeds and nuts (except peanuts and chestnuts, which are starches), cheese, and milk. Combine these with nonstarchy and ocean vegetables and sour fruits.
- **Acid fruits include** citrus fruits, pineapples, plums (sour), pomegranates, strawberries, and sour fruits.
- **Subacid fruits include** apples, apricots, cherries, grapes, mangoes, papayas, pears, and nectarines.
- **Sweet fruits include** bananas, dates, figs, prunes, raisins, and persimmons.
- **Avocado combines best with** nonstarchy/green vegetables and acid or subacid fruits.
- **Tomatoes combine best with** nonstarchy/green vegetables and protein.
- **Melons are best eaten without other foods** as they will digest quickly and easily when eaten alone.

NEXT STEPS

- Eat only when relaxed.
- Incorporate rituals of mindfulness before meals.
- Chew food until it is almost liquid.
- Eliminate trans fats from your diet.
- Ensure sufficient digestive enzymes.
- Identify each organ of digestion and ensure it is working well.
- Treat gut permeability.
- Eat a variety of prebiotic foods, including soluble and insoluble fibers.
- Eat a variety of probiotic "fermented" foods.
- Follow food combination principles for better digestion.

CHAPTER 5

The Rules of the Good Mood Kitchen

I have organized this book with attention to what I consider the foremost essentials of mood-savvy diet and nutrition. What follows are my recommendations for simple guidelines that will provide you with what you need for mood-savvy health. The list below is not an exhaustive one, but adhering to these main essentials—even in small ways—can have an enormously positive effect on your physical and emotional well-being.

1. Remember that no single diet is right for everyone.
Each person has a different cultural-genetic heritage and therefore a different metabolism. Some peoples—like the Inuit—require mostly meat and fish, whereas people from India do well on a predominance of legumes, vegetables, fruits, and grains. Most people require a mix. However, that mix of food can vary greatly. Know your ancestral and genetic heritage and try to eat for your individual metabolic type.

2. Eat all the colors of the "brainbow."
The *brainbow diet* is my term for a full-color-spectrum diet that nourishes the brain, mind, and body in order to enhance mental health. Eat whole, nutrient-dense foods from the entire color spectrum to obtain your nutrients. Each color brings different vitamins and healing nutrients to the brain (see the Colors of the "Brainbow" section in Resources for a comprehensive list). Prepare fresh foods daily.

3. Eat breakfast and maintain a "full" feeling throughout the day.
Eat a protein-rich breakfast every day. Protein and fats stabilize your mood.

Eating only carbohydrates allows you to feel energized at first, but then relaxation or even fatigue may set in. Eating fats provides a sense of feeling full.

Eliminate refined carbohydrates, especially from your breakfast. When your blood sugar drops, so does your mood. Do not allow yourself to become hungry.

4. Eat food that nourishes the brain _and_ the gut.

The brain is made up of 60% fat. It needs enough good-quality fat, proteins, and carbohydrates (sugar) to function. To improve mood, focus, attention, and memory, eat plenty of good fats like butter, eggs, avocados, walnuts, and coconut oil. The gut, the digestive system through which the body absorbs what it needs from the foods we eat, is the "second brain." Nourish your second brain with fiber and fermented foods, which will also generate the healthy bacteria and neurotransmitters that support efficient brain chemistry.

Poor-quality fats and trans fats, like the fat in French fries and the partially hydrogenated oils added to canned and packaged foods, should be eliminated from your diet.

5. Assess your physical and emotional state before you eat.

Eat only when relaxed. Digestion occurs when the parasympathetic nervous system is switched on. The juices in our body that contain digestive enzymes flow when we're in a state of relaxation.

We should never eat under stress. As tempting as a snack can be when we're at our most frazzled, eating under stress is like putting a pot of food on the stove to cook, not lighting the fire, and letting it sit there for two days. It bubbles, ferments, and becomes gaseous.

6. Listen to your gut.

Bodily discomforts, mood swings, low energy, and emotional challenges tell a story of your body's unique nutritional needs. By listening to your symptoms, you can make that story coherent and translate it into appropriate and effective dietary changes.

7. Use smart nutrition to balance the digestion and nutrition factors that underlie mental challenges.

Where there is mental illness or challenges with emotional balance, look for a history of digestive problems. Use nutrition to balance the five essential digestion and nutrition factors that underlie mental illness: (1) sleep and circadian rhythm, (2) blood sugar levels and hypoglycemia; (3) food allergies and sensitivities; (4) inflammation; and (5) oxidative stress and mitochondrial function. (More information about these factors—and how they apply to your diet—is provided in later chapters.)

8. Eliminate exposure to toxic substances.

Mental health is affected negatively by dietary exposure to food toxins and allergens. It is important to eliminate from your diet any food that contains additives, preservatives, hormones, toxic pesticides, and petrochemical fertilizers. They're more common than you might think.

Use wild foods and organic foods. If you cannot obtain these foods all the time, focus your attention on finding organic eggs and meat products, and detoxify your fruits and vegetables.

9. Remember that diet is essential, but diet alone is not sufficient.

To achieve steady mood regulation and overcome mental health challenges, it is essential to not only choose a healthy diet but also to incorporate regular use of vitamins, minerals, amino acids, and glandular supplements. A healthy diet is essential for overall mental health; however, it is not generally sufficient by itself to treat mental illness.

10. Choose healthy foods and nutrients over alcohol and harmful drugs to alter consciousness.

Foods and nutrients, alcohol, and drugs can all alter consciousness. Distinguish between altering consciousness for health or for addiction. Understand what is being altered in order to gain control over an addiction. Transform addiction into positive states of consciousness, linked to ceremonial and shared group activities.

11. Integrate change while making nutritional substitutions.

First integrate good habits, then replace bad habits. Personal change takes place by integrating positive activities (habits) first and then eliminating negative habits (activities). Identify one positive change behavior and its corresponding negative habit at a time. Substitute healthier foods that will satisfy the same needs.

PART 2

What You Need to Know

CHAPTER 6

What's Your Digestion Profile?
A Diet and Health
Self-Assessment Guide

You may have seen specialists for a variety of mental or physical health symptoms, but you still may wonder how to put the pieces together about the possible relationship between these symptoms, your nutrition, and your health. This next chapter will help you begin the journey to discover these relationships. You want to know why you feel the way you do, and what you can do about it. This is the first step to making these important health changes. Symptoms tell a story of nutritional and emotional challenges. When conducting your self-assessment, consider that it's like putting together a jigsaw puzzle. Some pieces may fit together right away, while others take a while to figure out. But with time and attention, you will soon begin to discern a pattern that makes sense. Start a journal where you keep track of your symptoms and responses to your dietary changes.

During a self-assessment, your goal is to identify:

1. The relationship between your mental health symptoms and nutrition.
2. Connections between mental and physical symptoms.
3. Both healthy and unhealthy food behaviors as an effort to reestablish balance in the system.
4. Alternatives to current unhealthy behaviors that will bring positive, lasting results.

5. Three nutritional goals to begin the change process.
6. The nature of your relationship to food.

YOUR PERSONAL PROFILE

Below I will guide you through some basic self-assessments that include both my own questionnaires, standard surveys, and laboratory tests that analyze blood, saliva, and hair. See the Resources section for where to order blood tests and other labs I suggest below.

There are four main areas to self-assess in developing a personal diet profile and an individualized nutritional plan for emotional balance:

1. Body clock
2. Blood sugar
3. Food sensitivities
4. Inflammation

Body Clock

If the "body clock" is out of balance, it contributes significantly to depression, anxiety, PTSD, chronic pain (fibromyalgia), menstrual problems, obsessive-compulsive disorder (OCD), bipolar disorder, eating disorders, and insomnia. Indeed, some illnesses are now considered to be primarily a result of a body clock that is either "delayed" or "advanced." Finding your natural rhythm will improve your health. Medications, nutrients, and light exposure can all affect—adversely or beneficially—the sleep-wake cycle and mood. Early-morning waking, morning depression, chronic sleeping in late, awakening with exhaustion, feeling wired at night, and using medication to sleep are all signs of circadian rhythm disruption.

Think of a major clock in the brain that is linked to the great planetary "clock" of daytime and nighttime, light and dark. This master clock then regulates other smaller clocks in the body that in turn regulate digestion, glucose handling, and hunger. Mood disorders occur when the "brain clock" is out of sync with the master clock of light and dark, and in turn this disrupts the way the smaller clocks are regulated. Thus, to reset these clocks so they are all synchronized, we use being awake, sleep therapies involving light and dark, and nutritional therapies that help move the "hands" of the clock backward or forward.

Stress alters the body clock rhythm via hormones such as cortisol, which in turn affect sleep, wakefulness, and fatigue. Sleep deprivation is a risk factor for the development of dementia. Night shift workers are more vulnerable to stress-related illnesses, including depression and anxiety.

One of the positive changes you can make is to "set" your body clock to improve your mood by light exposure along with nutrition and nutrients. This is called *chrononutrition*, which refers to the relationship between the timing of food intake and addressing nutrient deficits with specific vitamins. Diet supplementation and food behaviors can rebalance the circadian rhythm and thus contribute to improved mental health.

Possible Signs of 24-Hour Body Clock (Circadian Rhythm) Imbalance
Check next to each of these symptoms to assess if you will benefit from regulating your body clock:

✓ Insomnia
✓ Depression, especially early-morning waking depression
✓ PTSD
✓ Bipolar disorder
✓ Premenstrual syndrome
✓ Bulimia
✓ Dementia
✓ Fibromyalgia
✓ Awakening in the morning feeling exhausted
✓ Sleeping late

WAYS TO ASSESS MY BODY CLOCK RHYTHM

1. Fill out the self-assessment survey at the following website:

Center for Environmental Therapeutics (http://www.cet.org/)

2. Take a 24-hour salivary cortisol test at the following website:

http://www.lef.org/Vitamins-Supplements/Blood-Tests

Ways to Align My Body Clock
Now that you know more about your 24-hour circadian rhythm, what are some actions you can take?

Make sure you get natural light exposure every morning or at noon time for at least 20 minutes. Don't wear your sunglasses but allow indirect light to be seen and absorbed.

Use the following brain-savvy nutrients to balance the body clock:

- Vitamin B-12 (sublingual methylcobalamin), 1 mg/day
- Melatonin (use at night), 0.5 mg/day

Wear blue light blocking glasses at night about 1 or 2 hours before going to bed. Even if you are watching TV or on the computer, wear these glasses so the melatonin can kick in.

If you are going to bed after midnight on a regular basis (and you are not a shift worker), begin to go to bed 10 minutes earlier. Make these changes over the course of a month or so until you are going to sleep no later than 11:00 p.m.

Use coffee to awaken in the morning but not after 12 noon.

Blood Sugar

After the body clock, the next most important function to assess is blood sugar handling, reactive hypoglycemia (abnormally low blood sugar), and hyperglycemia (excessive blood sugar) or diabetes. Most people with mood swings have poor blood sugar handling. Hypoglycemia causes significant mood swings that can appear to be anxiety, bipolar disorder, irritability, or attention deficit hyperactivity disorder (ADHD). People with chronic stress often experience low blood sugar following a meal (reactive hypoglycemia).

Possible Signs of Reactive Hypoglycemia
Ask yourself whether you experience the following:

- ✓ Mood swings
- ✓ Irritability
- ✓ Hunger or cravings
- ✓ Shakiness, or feeling "rubbery," or about to faint between meals
- ✓ Feeling lightheaded or dizzy
- ✓ Confusion

✓ Being easily provoked to anger
✓ Inability to concentrate or focus
✓ Anxiety
✓ Sleepiness after meals or at times during the day

Score: If you checked 5 symptoms or more, it is important to investigate whether your blood sugar handling is contributing to your symptoms.

ASSESS MY BLOOD SUGAR

You can further assess blood sugar handling in 3 ways:
- Food-Mood diary
- Fasting blood glucose (blood test)
- HbA1c (blood test)

Ask your health provider, or obtain a test requisition at a lab listed in the Resources section.

FOOD-MOOD DIARY AND CHECKLIST

The food-mood diary and checklist is the first place to start your food-mood self-assessment, and it will also help you to assess how you handle blood sugar (glucose). It provides a 3-day window into food habits and patterns. It allows you to identify patterns of mood and energy and how they may be connected to food quality, quantity, and timing of intake. It is the first step in the jigsaw puzzle and will provide you with ideas of where to start the change process.

Food-Mood Diary

Name: _____   Date: _____

Write down everything you eat and drink for 3 days, including all snacks, beverages, and water. Please include approximate amounts. Describe your energy, mood or digestive responses associated with a meal/snack, and record them in the right-hand column. Use an up arrow (↑) for an increase in energy/mood, a down arrow (↓) for a decrease in energy/mood, and an equal sign (=) if energy/mood is unchanged.

Time of waking: _____ a.m. / p.m.

Meal	Beverages	Energy level (↑,↓, or =)	Mood (↑,↓, or =)	Digestive response (gas, bloating, gurgling, elimination, etc.)
Breakfast (time: _____)				
Snacks (time: _____)				
Lunch (time: _____)				
Snacks (time: _____)				
Dinner (time: _____)				
Snacks (time: _____)				

After you fill out the diary, you can review it step by step with the following checklist, filling in the answers and identifying the changes you want to make.

Self-Care Checklist for the Food-Mood Diary		
Question	Response	Goals and recommendations
1. How much time passed between when you woke up and when you ate breakfast? Are you eating breakfast?		One should always eat breakfast, containing at least 3–4 ounces of protein within 60 minutes of waking for proper energy and blood sugar balancing.
2. How much water/broth are you drinking throughout the day?		Water intake should be about 50% of body weight every day in ounces (if you weigh 160 lb., for example, you should be drinking 80 ounces of water daily).
3. How often are you eating? How many hours between each meal or snack?		Food should be eaten every 3–4 hours to prevent mood swings, and you will benefit from at least 3 meals/day and 2 snacks.
4. How many servings of vegetables are you eating per day?		At least 3 servings of vegetables should be eaten every day. A serving equals from ½ to 1 cup.
5. Are you eating raw vegetables and fruits?		At least 1–3 servings of raw fruit or vegetables should be eaten every day.
6. Are you eating enough protein? Note if lack of protein corresponds to drops in mood.		Proteins help to stabilize energy and balance mood and should be emphasized during the daytime hours.
7. Are you eating enough fats? Note if lack of fats corresponds to mood shifts.		Fats help to stabilize energy and balance mood and should be emphasized during the daytime hours.
8. How many servings of starchy carbohydrates are you eating, and at what times of day?		During the day carbohydrates are best when combined with protein; carbohydrates alone can be emphasized in the evening for relaxation.
9. What is the quality of the food you are eating (freshly prepared vs. canned or prepackaged foods)?		Emphasize whole, fresh, organic foods over packaged and canned foods.
10. Are you eating enough fiber?		Fiber is found in foods like fruits and vegetable skins, oat bran, nuts, beans, lentils, psyllium husk, peas, chia seeds, barley, and some fruits and vegetables. Men should be eating about 38 grams/day, and women 25 grams/day.

After you complete the checklist, make a list of three goals you have identified and how you will prioritize them. Remember that it is important is to make a change that you feel you can do right now. Don't try to make changes that you don't feel ready for. Give yourself an opportunity to be successful.

Make a list of your goals. Some of the goals you make might include:

- Eat 1–2 eggs for breakfast.
- Increase the amount of water by 4 glasses a day.
- Substitute real organic cream for creamer.
- Use healthy fat (olive oil) on salad.
- Add protein to a lunch salad.
- Obtain low-acid coffee.
- Use a natural sweetener like stevia or honey instead of artificial sweetener.
- Substitute apples instead of applesauce.
- Substitute peanut butter and dark cocoa for candy.
- Reduce or eliminate soft drinks.
- Buy a Crock-Pot to cook easy recipes.

Food Sensitivities

Food allergies and sensitivities can contribute to mood swings and to mental distress. It is important to identify what you are allergic to or what you suspect and want to confirm with further testing. Review some major culprits below and how to assess if you are reactive to them.

Gluten/casein

Celiac disease, non-celiac gluten sensitivity, and casein sensitivity are all important causes of mental illness. Significant clinical evidence has established casein and gluten sensitivity in people with mood disorders, anxiety, major depression, schizophrenia, bipolar disorder, OCD, autism, ADHD, and eating disorders.

Gluten is the protein found in certain grains (wheat, barley, and rye) that causes grains to "glue" together. Gliadins are proteins that are components of gluten. Celiac disease affects about 1 in 250 people and is an autoimmune disease that manifests in severe digestive and frequently neu-rological symptoms. Non-celiac gluten sensitivity is an immune response leading to both digestive and neurological problems but may not manifest in digestive distress and thus may go undiagnosed.

Casein is the protein found in dairy milk products. Both gluten and casein contain proteins to which people may be either allergic or sensitive. About 50% of people who are sensitive to gluten are sensitive to casein. This is called "cross reactivity."

Gluten and Casein Self-Assessment

There are two basic approaches to assessment—one you can do yourself at home, called the elimination diet, and one that involves blood and/or salivary tests. Testing for both celiac and the various antibodies to gliadin and other gluten protein, or an elimination diet, should be enacted as a first step.

There are different tests for non-celiac gluten sensitivity; one assesses blood and the other saliva. There are many types of gliadins or gluten pro-teins in grains, and simple salivary tests may miss these reactions in people with non-celiac gluten sensitivity.

Adherence to a gluten- and casein-free diet is challenging for many people, especially children. Thus, it is important to conduct highly spe-cific testing. New tests are available for both urine and blood serum which expand immune system testing to include the testing of peptides, which act as undigested proteins that contribute to gastrointestinal, neurological, and neurodevelopmental disorders. These neuropeptides, called casomorphins and gliadorphins, act like opiates in the brain; they affect cognitive function, speech, and auditory integration and decrease the ability to feel pain. For example, bingeing associated with bulimia is linked to gluten sensitivity, which releases opioid peptides, which accounts for the binging/withdrawal response to grains, especially wheat. Cravings for wheat and grains are often associated with mood elevation upon eating these foods. See the Resources section for labs that test for gluten and casein sensitivities.

TRY THIS!

Skin Brushing

Bulimia and eating disorders in general are often associated with a history of early-life trauma. This leads to feelings of being "out of the body," or dissociation. If you are sensitive to Gluten, it exacerbates dissociation. An effective self-care behavior to support your nutritional change from eating disorders like bulimia is skin brushing. Skin brushing is best done in the morning upon awakening and in the early evening, just before bathing, but it can be done at any time of day when you will feel the benefits.

Buy a natural bristle skin brush.

I love the Yerba Prima brand, which can be used with or without its long handle. Skin brushing is done when the skin is dry, not wet. Always sweep in the direction of the heart. Begin at one of the feet and in long strokes sweep up the front of the leg, calf to thigh, then reach around back and sweep up the back of the calf, thigh, and buttocks to the lower back. Do a set of 3 fully complete sweeps in each area. Now do this on the opposite side of the body. When the legs have been done, lift one arm over your head and sweep down from the wrist, moving down the inner arm and gently passing over the underarm and the breast tissue, being careful not to touch the nipple. Then sweep the outside of the arm and up over the shoulders toward the neck.

Cover all areas on the arm three times, then repeat on the other arm. Now, gently, brush from the bottom of the neck over the chest and sternum in the direction of the heart, and, next, sweep up along the abdomen in the direction of the heart. When you are finished, take a moment to close your eyes and feel the various sensations you are experiencing, breathing rhythmically and allowing the experience to bring you into body awareness. (Korn, 2012)

Inflammation

Chronic inflammation consists of low-level but persistent inflammation. It is not the same as having an acute bruise or swelling that heals in a few days. Depression, autism, schizophrenia, fibromyalgia, and chronic fatigue are all linked to low levels of inflammation.

After you assess your levels of inflammation you can focus on lowering intake of inflammatory foods and increasing the use of non–inflammatory foods.

ASSESS MY LEVELS OF INFLAMMATION

1. What is my ACE Score?

ACE refers to *Adverse Childhood Events*. It is well known that having higher levels of adverse childhood events makes one vulnerable to inflammatory processes that lead to chronic pain, depression, and illness. Knowing your vulnerability and your score can help you obtain the help and support you need to reduce inflammation at its source. Food and nutrients can either help or hurt inflammation. You can take the quiz by searching online for "Find my ACE score."

2. C-reactive protein (CRP) is a marker that defines a general level of inflammation in the body.

3. High cholesterol may be a reaction to inflammation in the body. Include this analysis as part of your assessment.

4. Do I have pain in my body and if so where? Might this indicate chronic inflammation?

5. Take 3 vital supplements to address inflammation:
   - Proteolytic enzymes
   - Turmeric (curcumin)
   - Fish oil and borage oil

Food Preparation Exercise
- Make a list of the current ways you access and prepare food.
- Make a list of new methods you want to learn to prepare foods.
- Jot down any obstacles to implementing the new methods and how you hope to resolve them.

Diet History

Your diet history and early influences can provide insight into your current status today. One exercise is to write an account of your dietary history and practices, describing where you have come from, where you are now, and where you wish to go.

You might explore the foods you ate as a child—including addictive foods, fats and oils, proteins, carbs, sweets, and comfort foods.

- Were you breastfed, or did you drink formula?
- Did you have ear infections and use antibiotics (and thus experience possible effects on the gut)?

- Did you complain of stomachaches? (Besides stress, stomachaches might reflect allergies to dairy or gluten.)
- Were you a "latchkey kid"?
- Did you cook for yourself or your siblings?
- Was there fighting at mealtime?
- Were foods prepared from packages or homemade, or were they special types of meals? Were you a vegetarian?
- Was your diet based on religious or spiritual beliefs?

Where have you already made positive changes? Where may you still want to make changes?

MEDICATIONS, NUTRIENTS, AND HERBS

First, make a list of all the medications, vitamins, minerals and supplements, and any herbs that you use. It is essential to identify all use of medications, including prescription, self-prescribed, and recreational or abused medications. Why is this important? One reason is that there can be complex drug-nutrient-herb interactions. For example, fish oil is a blood thinner; if you are already taking a blood thinner, it is important to know this information. Often you might see different clinicians who may suggest different medications or nutrients. Having a complete list helps you and your providers make informed decisions.

Medications Self-Assessment

Consider 4 types of substances to alter mood and overall health:

- Prescription medications
- Over the counter (OTC) medications
- Self-prescribed drugs or medications
- Self-prescribed nutritional supplements

In the table below, list any medications, including pharmaceuticals and antibiotics, that you are currently or have previously taken.

Medication	Prescribed for	Dosage	Frequency	Prescribed by (doctor's name / self)
E.g., Wellbutrin	Depression	100 mg	2/day	Dr. Morry

Now list the non-pharmaceutical substances you have taken:

Use of Non-Pharmaceutical Substances			
Current	Past	Substance	Times per week/Comments
		tobacco	
		alcohol/drugs	
		coffee/soda	
		cannabis	
		NutraSweet (aspartame)	
		other	

In the table below, list any nutritional supplements—including vitamins, minerals, herbs, and amino acids—that you are currently or have previously taken.

Supplement	Manufacturer	Dosage	Frequency	Dates/Duration
e.g., Vitamin C	Biotics Research,Inc	500 mg	2/day	4 months

Next, review each medication by entering it an online database (or referring to a book) to see if there are influences that may cause nutritional deficits. Compare to see the interactions that may occur when taking medications, and nutrients and herbs, and assess where you might make changes to prevent side effects. Discuss with a practitioner how to address these deficits.

DRUG-HERB-NUTRIENT DATABASES

- Website: http://reference.medscape.com/drug-interactionchecker
- Website: http://www.webmd.com/interaction-checker/

HEIGHT AND WEIGHT, HEADACHES, SKIN CONDITIONS, AND PAIN

Height and Weight

Some of the things that people worry about the most include what they weigh and the number for their body mass index (BMI). BMI is a rough measure of body fat based on height and weight that applies to adult men and women. Although the BMI is commonly used, it is not particularly meaningful to health. Instead of the BMI or weight per se, consider the hip-waist ratio as a more effective tool *if* you require a measure.

Action: Focus on aerobic conditioning and strength training for mental well-being, and choose activities that improve overall well-being, with less focus on weight per se.

HIP-WAIST RATIO

To accurately measure the waist and hip ratio, follow these steps:
- Place a tape measure around your bare stomach just above the upper hipbone.
- Make sure the measuring tape is parallel to the floor (slanting can falsely increase your measurement). Also ensure that the tape measure is snug to your body, but not so tight that it compresses the skin. Exhale while measuring, and relax your abdomen—sucking in is not allowed!
- Using a tape measure, measure the circumference of your hips.
- First look in a mirror and identify the widest part of your buttocks. Then place the tape measure at this location and measure around the circumference of your hips and buttocks.

Using your waist circumference measurement, calculate your waist-to-hip ratio by dividing your waist circumference by your hip measurement; a result above 0.9 for men or 0.85 for women indicates abdominal obesity and an elevated health risk.

Headaches

Do you have headaches? What types and how often, and what seems to trigger incidents? Gluten and food allergies are major triggers for headaches. Sinus headaches may signify food allergies, especially to dairy. Dehydration can also cause headaches, as can muscle tension and anxiety. Be aware that using medications for headaches can cause digestive problems.

Skin Conditions

Do you have acne, dermatitis, eczema, chronic rashes, or fungal infections? These may indicate an allergy to dairy products and sensitivity to sugar, along with low essential fatty acid levels.

Pain

Joint pain and muscle aches may reflect sensitivity to nightshade foods, gluten, and casein.

DIGESTION/ELIMINATION BODY SCAN TO IDENTIFY PROBLEM AREAS IN YOUR BODY

You can begin with the following guided meditation to explore where you may be having problems with digestion and elimination.

Consider any challenges you have had in the past or that you now have with your digestion. Think of digestion as a process that travels from North to South—starting at your head and traveling downward. Close your eyes, and focus your breathing, and do a body scan. A body scan allows you to use your "inner eye" to feel and see how each organ feels and what sensations it holds. Begin by breathing deeply, and focus your attention on your skull and the brain inside. Continue to breath rhythmically as you make a mental note of any feelings or sensations. Continue to direct and follow your attention to your mouth, then your jaw, the throat, down the esophagus—taking your time, breathing and paying attention as you breathe . . . exploring the stomach, then the liver and gallbladder, the small intestine, the pancreas, the large intestines, and then elimination via the rectum. You may find that you spend more time in some areas than others. That's OK. Allow your attention and your inner eye to reveal the wisdom of your awareness. When you have finished this leisurely journey, open your eyes and then jot down some notes about the areas where you experienced distress or imbalance. Below are just a few places to begin your journey of personal nutritional self-discovery.

The Brain

Addictions are a brain-mind-body issue, often related to nutrient deficits or to self- medicating pain or discomfort. They are best helped by eliminating addictive foods, nourishing the brain and body with vitamins, minerals, and amino acids, and by adopting a high-quality, higher-fat diet.

The Mouth and Jaw

We begin to digest starchy carbohydrates by chewing them and generating saliva. Ideally, the jaw moves rhythmically to chew our food to near liquid form before we swallow it. However, if we are stressed or tense our jaw can be so tight or painful that we neglect to adequately chew our food. Problems like this can be addressed with stress reduction or bodywork techniques that release muscle tension. Gum disease can also contribute to nutritional problems, as pain and tooth loss can lead to chewing challenges. If our mouths hurt, we may avoid raw foods and thus lose access to important nutrients. Bad breath is a sign of gum disease and/or fermentation in the stomach or small intestine. You can help to eliminate bad breath and prevent or treat gum disease by using 100 mg CoQ_{10} a day and by using the ancient Ayurvedic remedy "oil pulling."

TRY THIS!

Oil Pulling

Both the bacteria streptococcus mutans and the yeast Candida albicans live in the mouth and can multiply and cause tooth decay and gum disease, especially when there is a high starch or sugar diet. During oil pulling, the oil acts as a detergent and pulls bacteria from the mouth as it also protects the gums.

Take 1–2 tablespoons of raw coconut oil or raw sesame oil into your mouth every night before bed. Swish it in your mouth for 10 minutes and then spit it out. You will need to do this nightly for several months before seeing improvements, but it is well worth the commitment.

Esophagus, stomach

Symptoms of burning or sharp pain in the upper chest and throat can signify a common problem called gastroesophageal reflux disease (GERD). This often results from a combination of indigestion, high sugar diet, and stress. It is also called "heartburn" because it can feel like a fire in the chest and neck, or even a heart attack.

Liver

If you have persistent pain on the right side under the ribs it might mean some type of liver disease that should be professionally assessed. Fatty liver disease can come from a lifetime of poor-quality fats or from alcohol-related toxicity. Fortunately, the liver can often respond very well to dietary changes outlined in this book. One of the best herbs for aiding the liver is milk thistle.

Gallbladder

The old adage "fat, female, forty and fertile" refers to the propensity of fat, fertile, 40-year old women to develop gallstones and to be assessed for them if they have abdominal pain, especially on the right side. However, I have seen plenty of gallstones and sludge in thin women, menopausal women, men, and even in children. Luckily, the gallbladder will readily release the sludge and stones if given the chance nutritionally. And don't forget to eat good-quality fats; it's a myth that one must reduce fats in the diet—quite the opposite. Eliminate bad fats and eat plenty of good ones. You can also use the product Beta-TCP to support your gallbladder.

Small intestines

If you draw a 2-inch square outward around your belly button and gently press around the perimeter you can feel your small intestines. If you feel any pain in that area, you may also be experiencing digestive problems.

HOW TO MASSAGE MY ILEOCECAL VALVE, AND WHAT DOES IT DO?

To assess your ileocecal valve, place your right thumb on your navel (belly button), your right little finger on your right hip (the high part of your pelvic bone). Imagine a line connecting those two points. Then locate the middle of that line with your left middle finger and allow it to rest in the middle. Now release your right hand and use it to press that midway point until you feel a little discomfort. That's the ileocecal valve; it's the important sphincter that meets at the small and large intestine and allows food to pass through to the large intestine without backing up into the small intestine again. Improving digestion through diet and gentle daily massage of this area can alleviate any pain in this area and improve the function of this important valve.

Large intestines (colon)

Among the major symptoms of an unhappy colon are diarrhea or constipation, and sometimes both in an alternating cycle. There may also be painful gas and bloating. Any of these symptoms indicate that help is necessary in order to aid digestion and elimination. While our food waste is processed, stored, and finally eliminated from the colon, our "emotional waste" also tends to reside in the colon, disposed of and forgotten until we can no longer ignore it.

To help your colon function and feel better, remember that it thrives on plenty of probiotics and prebiotics, some of which are available in apples—hence the saying, "An apple a day keeps the doctor away."

Rectum

A common problem that occurs at the end of the North-to-South journey is hemorrhoids. Hemorrhoids can be painful. Increasing fiber and water in your diet is essential, as are sitz baths in warm water and oatmeal. Drinking slipper elm bark tea is also very soothing.

This self-assessment and body scan of the digestive organs will help to start you on the road to a healing diet. However, don't rely on this self-assessment alone. If you suspect a problem or you have unexplained or persistent pain, contact your practitioner and bring your notes and observations with you.

ANTICIPATE OBSTACLES AND FOCUS ON STRENGTHS

Identify the differing needs within your current family; Will you encounter obstacles to changing your diet and method of food preparation, or adding in new recipes? If so, what might they be, and what steps can you take to resolve those issues?

NEXT STEPS

- Assess your body clock/circadian rhythm
- Assess your blood sugar handling
- Assess your inflammation levels
- List all medications, supplements, and remedies
- Write up a diet history
- Complete a body scan and self-assessment of organs of digestion
- Identify any new tests you need to obtain to complete your assessment
- Identify any obstacles to making changes

Troubleshoot Food-Mood Connections: Nutritional Culprits Behind Depression, Addictions, and Other Challenges

If you currently experience depression, anxiety, and worry; sleep or focus problems; or addictions to drugs, alcohol, or foods; there are ways to significantly improve your health and well-being through the use of foods and supplemental nutrients. High-quality nutrient dense foods and nutritional support often provide the missing key to attaining mental well-being. Nutritional problems can also occur due to poor digestion, however, despite following a healthy diet. If you have chronic digestive problems, it is likely that these problems also contribute to mental distress. In this chapter I provide some ways to "connect the dots" between nutritional deficits and poor mental health, along with some recipes to address these imbalances.

DEPRESSION AND LOW MOOD

Depression often occurs after a long period of stress. Stress also leads to inflammation and nutritional imbalance, which in turn contribute to depression.

Vitamin and mineral deficiencies are common among people who are depressed. In particular, deficiencies include the B vitamins (biotin, folic acid, B_6, B_1, and B_{12}), vitamin C, and the minerals calcium, copper, iron, magnesium, potassium, and zinc. However, excessive levels of lead and copper (obtained from drinking well water, for example) can also contribute to depression.

People who are anxious and depressed often have low levels of magnesium, but too much calcium can also contribute to depression; this is why older people with osteoporosis should take calcium supplements only under professional guidance. Vitamin D deficiency is also an important factor in depression; therefore, vitamin D levels should be checked yearly with a blood test.

Women are vulnerable to depression associated with perimenopause or menopause, in part because hormonal changes lower neurotransmitter levels. As estrogen levels decrease, serotonin levels can decrease as well. Progesterone deficiency at this stage is common not only because of the stage of life but also because stress depletes progesterone. Bioidentical progesterone can improve mood and aid sleep.

It is important to recognize that testosterone levels affect the health of both men and women. Low levels of vitamin D and zinc contribute to low testosterone, as do statins and environmental toxins like herbicides. Supplementation of bioidentical testosterone functions as an antidepressant in men who have low or borderline testosterone levels.

Depression and mood disorders often begin with chronic stress. The stress response is mediated largely via the adrenal glands. If you nourish the adrenal glands midday with good-quality protein topped with sea salt, you will begin to balance your body clock and blood sugar, which helps to regulate mood.

Seasonal Affective Disorder

Seasonal affective disorder is a specific type of depression and low mood associated with lack of sunlight during the winter. Also known as "winter depression," it generally improves when the sun returns in the spring and summer. It occurs more often in women. Symptoms of SAD include difficulty waking up in the morning, oversleeping, fatigue, low mood, craving for carbohydrates, and weight gain.

TRY THIS!

Eat lunch outside, and ditch the sunglasses.

Eat lunch outside daily during the winter months, weather permitting, and don't wear sunglasses. Even on overcast days, the natural light will enter your eyes and stimulate your brain, thus helping to counter seasonal affective disorder (SAD).

The key to reducing the symptoms of SAD is getting enough light and nutrients that support circadian rhythm. Getting enough light involves sitting in front of a light box every morning, moving to the tropics, or eating lunch outside every day around noon. I created the following recipe to ensure that you eat enough protein, fat, and carbohydrates, which can help to reduce the symptoms of SAD. It is also rich in chlorophyll, which helps transport light in the cells.

Winter Mood Bean Boost: Savory White Beans and Saffron

This dish is a perfect mood booster for a dreary winter day. Saffron, which is derived from the crocus flower, is the antidepressant centerpiece of this recipe, along with beans that are rich in B vitamins.

Ingredients

2 lb. dried large white beans

5 qt. water

3 bay leaves

4 tbsp. virgin olive oil

2 large white onions, finely diced

3 cloves garlic, finely chopped

½ c. finely chopped flat leaf parsley

1 c. of organic spinach

1 tsp. saffron threads

Sea salt and ground black pepper, to taste

Directions

1. Soak beans overnight in water in the fridge.
2. Drain the soaked beans. Place in a large pot with fresh water, bring to a boil, and reduce heat. Simmer for 2 hours with bay leaves.
3. Heat virgin olive oil in a sauté pan over medium heat. Add onions and garlic and sauté for 3 minutes. Add spinach, parsley and saffron, and cook for 1 minute more, then remove from heat.
4. Drain the cooked beans of most of the excess water. Return the beans to the pot and add cooked onion/garlic/saffron mixture. Stir and add sea salt and black pepper to taste.

Variation: Try adding steamed white fish (cod, halibut, etc.) to this recipe, which can be added to the stew at the end, or set on top of the beans when served.

MOOD SWINGS

People with mood swings or bipolar disorder often have food sensitivities, such as to gluten and casein, and are sensitive to artificial sweeteners such as aspartame. Low blood sugar, or hypoglycemia, also aggravates mood swings. People with mood swings and bipolar disorder will benefit from good-quality fats in their diet and eating the hypoglycemic diet.

Mood swings are made worse when blood sugar drops. Make sure you do not get hungry, and eat a small amount of protein, fats, and carbohydrates every 3 hours during the day and into the evening. Have on hand ingredients to make a quick smoothie. Here are two recipes that provide stable energy and clear thinking, quickly.

Brain Focus Smoothie

This smoothie provides foods that are rich in lutein, which enhances brain function (and eye sight) and improves focus, concentration, and processing speed. While it is ideal if all the ingredients are organic, the spinach must be organic, as non-organic spinach retains pesticides more than most vegetables. Make this smoothie for breakfast or as a snack when you need to apply some high-speed brain power, and then chew on some pecans or walnuts in between smoothie sips.

Ingredients

1–2 ripe kiwi
½ ripe avocado
½ cup fresh organic spinach leaves
½ cup coconut cream or coconut milk
1 organic egg yolk
½ cup of hemp milk
1 tablespoon raw honey

Freeze the hemp and coconut milk in ice cube trays in advance if you like this smoothie cold. Peel the kiwi and avocado, and mix together with all the ingredients in a blender until thick and frothy.

Pineapple-Coconut Cognitive Smoothie

This recipe is easy to make and satisfying for people of all ages who want to support cognitive function by feeding the brain nutrients and fats it can easily use for fuel.

Ingredients

1 c. frozen or fresh pineapple

½ c. coconut milk

1 c. coconut cream

1 tbsp. coconut oil

10 drops stevia liquid, or 1 tsp raw honey

Directions

Blend all ingredients and serve cold.

Variations

Frozen mango or blueberries also go well with pineapple and can be substituted for part of the pineapple. For example, you can use ½ cup of pineapple and 1 cup of mango or ½ cup of blueberries. Another option is to substitute 2 heaping tablespoons of pure cocoa for the fruit.

WORRY AND ANXIETY

Anxiety causes disruption in the natural rhythms of breathing. Shallow breathing and hyperventilation can cause headaches, neck pain, jaw pain, leg and body cramps, and tension in the shoulders and chest. Some signs of imbalanced breathing include sighing, breath holding, erratic breathing, and intermittent long sighs or gasps.

TRY THIS!

Worry and anxiety respond well to the combination of yoga, breathing exercises, and the generous use of organic apple cider vinegar. If you don't have a chance to add vinegar to your diet, place a cup in your bathtub water at night and soak, or add some to a plastic pail and do a foot soak for 20 minutes. You will feel relaxed and refreshed.

Shallow breathing depletes magnesium and contributes to anxiety, and anxiety causes shallow breathing. Anxiety is also associated with low levels of the neurotransmitter gamma-aminobutyric acid (GABA), a relaxing brain chemical that is inhibited by caffeine. Diet pills, amphetamines, asthma medication, caffeine, antihistamines, and steroids can increase anxiety and panic. Anxiety can also be exacerbated by a vegetarian diet, especially if you are a natural carnivore. If you are a vegetarian who is anxious and worries a lot, experiment with adding meat broth and apple cider vinegar to your diet for 4 weeks to see if your anxiety decreases and your mood lifts.

Pumpkin seeds are rich in magnesium and thus can calm anxiety. They are a good snack for someone with ADHD because they are high in good fats and zinc. They are also a good source of tryptophan, which is calming and aids sleep.

Always buy raw organic pumpkin seeds. You can eat them raw by the handful, or lightly pan-fry them in coconut oil, or season them with wheat-free tamari, and add a pinch of cayenne pepper for an energy boost. The seeds can also be added to a smoothie, or to a granola, or to a raw nut/seed mix for an on-the-go snack for children and adults alike.

LOW ENERGY AND CHRONIC FATIGUE

Adrenal fatigue underlies depression, anxiety, chronic pain, insomnia, and PTSD. Adrenal fatigue occurs in response to chronic stress. Imagine trying to drive a car with your foot on the accelerator while the car is in neutral. Eventually this will cause the engine to wear down and burn out. When the adrenal glands are repeatedly overstimulated by prolonged stress, poor diet, and excess caffeine, they tire out too.

DID YOU KNOW?

Eating protein such as eggs with raw butter and a generous amount of sea salt can reduce fatigue. Add alpha lipoic acid, CoQ_{10}, and D-ribose to your nutrient protocol for 3 months and observe the increase in energy. These foods and nutrients nourish your adrenal glands and the mitochondria—the "little engines" of the body.

Cortisol is a hormone secreted by the adrenal glands that is associated with stress. Under normal conditions cortisol levels are high in the morning, decrease during the day, and are lowest in the evening before sleep. In adrenal fatigue, however, the opposite can occur, which can result in a feeling of depression.

If you feel depressed, sluggish, and fatigued, have a difficult time awakening and getting active in the morning, and always feel cold—especially with cold hands and feet—you should also be assessed for thyroid function, which can be mistaken for a mood disorder.

TRY THIS!

Thyroid Boost—3-Course Menu
- Wild salmon
- Honey seaweed carrots
- Red lettuce with garlic yogurt dressing

6 oz. of lightly broiled wild salmon

Sprinkle sea salt and a little olive oil on the salmon, and place it on a cookie sheet. Bake for 10 minutes at 350 degrees, then place it on broil for the last 5 minutes. Keep a close eye on the salmon. It should be very pink on the inside.

Honey Seaweed Carrots

Seaweed is a rich source of iodine and thyroid support. This recipe nourishes and supports your endocrine system

Ingredients

1 pound of carrots

2 tbsp. unsalted raw butter

¼ tsp. dried French tarragon

Four drops stevia liquid

1 tbsp. raw honey

4 sheets of nori seaweed

sea salt and pepper to taste

Directions

1. Peel the carrots and cut into halves and quarters of equal size.
2. Heat a cast-iron pan on medium, and slowly melt the butter.
3. Place the cut and quartered carrots in the pan and let cook on a low heat for 10 minutes or until just tender.
4. Cut the sheets of nori with a sharp knife into 2-inch squares, or tear to approximate size
5. Add tarragon, stevia, honey and nori to the carrots and stir to mix them well. When all ingredients are fully integrated, turn out onto a serving dish and serve immediately. Top with fresh ground pepper and sea salt.

Red Lettuce With Garlic Yogurt Dressing

Ingredients

½ cup plain whole milk yogurt (goat milk, cow milk, or coconut yogurt)

4 tbsp. goat chevre (cheese made from goat's milk)

4 tbsp. organic olive oil or homemade mayonnaise

1 small garlic clove, minced

¼ tsp. dried or fresh basil

½ tbsp. organic apple cider vinegar

1 tsp. chopped fresh parsley

1 tsp. kelp flakes

2 stevia drops

Directions

Whisk all ingredients together in a bowl and serve as a dip for raw vegetables or as a dressing over lettuce and arugula. Remember, limit the raw cruciferous vegetables (broccoli, cauliflower Brussels sprouts) if you have an underactive thyroid.

SLEEP CHALLENGES AND INSOMNIA

We know that a good mood is dependent on a balanced body clock and the amount of quality sleep one obtains. Sleep improves mood, and improved mood helps sleep. There are many factors that contribute to poor sleep: disruption of the circadian rhythm cycle due to stress, certain medications and drugs, hypoglycemia, and low levels of B-vitamins, GABA, and serotonin.

Work to eliminate prescription sleep medications; although they allow you to sleep, they appear to affect memory negatively.

Restore your sleep and you will restore your mood and sense of well-being. Our ancient ancestors woke up with the sun and went to sleep with the dark. If you currently go to sleep late, try shifting your sleep time by 5 minutes every few days until you go to bed earlier and wake up earlier.

TRY THIS!

Enhance your sleep with 4 easy steps.

An hour before bed,

1. Take an Epsom salt bath.
2. Place "blue light blocking glasses" over your eyes.
3. Eat a small bowl of Oatmeal sprinkled with a tablespoon containing chopped walnuts, raisins, and pumpkin seeds. If you drink cow's milk, add ½ cup of warm raw milk to the bowl; otherwise use hemp milk.
4. Drink a cup of warm chamomile tea.

TRAUMA AND TRAUMA-RELATED STRESS

People who have been traumatized often experience depression, anxiety, insomnia, and dissociation along with intractable physical symptoms, such as chronic pain and problems associated with digestions, heart, breathing, and reproduction. Substance abuse, eating disorders, self-injury, and traumatic brain injury are also common among trauma victims.

TRY THIS!

As you know, healthy digestion occurs when one is relaxed. Stress, Anxiety, and PTSD make us vulnerable to acid indigestion and GERD. To ease GERD and a hiatal hernia, place an ice pack on the upper abdomen directly in the center—at the diaphragm below the ribs—for 15 minutes before eating. Also, drink licorice tea, which is an excellent tea for people with PTSD, as it soothes digestion and supports adrenal function.

The major nutritional factors affecting PTSD are similar to those in chronic depression and anxiety. Nutritional deficits can result from poor dietary habits associated with impaired self-care; from the side effects of pharmaceuticals to treat fibromyalgia, migraines, and irritable bowel syndrome; and from long-term effects of substance abuse.

TRY THIS!

Gelatin-Hemp Smoothie

Gelatin is comprised of the amino acids proline and glycine and is the protein building block for connective tissue and joints; these amino acids also support healthy mood, are anti-inflammatory, and are very easy to digest. Under the stress of trauma, it may be challenging to get good-quality protein and digest large meals; this smoothie answers that need. Hemp is especially good for PTSD recovery; hemp seed oil is rich in omega-3s and omega-6s and supports the endocannabinoid system in the brain. Turn to this gelatin-hemp smoothie once a day. (It's important to obtain grass-fed organic beef gelatin.) Feel free to vary the fruits in this smoothie.

Ingredients

1 c. of organic hemp milk

1 heaping tbsp. coconut oil or cold pressed hemp oil

½ c. of blueberries

1 frozen banana

2 tbsp. of gelatin

Directions

Place ingredients in the blender in the order they appear in the list. (Blend the gelatin first in a small amount of room-temperature—or warm—water, and then add it in as the last ingredient, to ensure a smooth blend.)

Note: You can also use hemp seeds in the smoothie as a substitute for the oil, but the oil has more nutritional value per ounce.

ADDICTION AND SUBSTANCE USE

Humans everywhere seek to alter their consciousness. Alcohol, drugs, psychotropic medications, plants, and foods all alter consciousness. Distinguishing between altering consciousness as a ritual for healing and for self-medication is essential for well-being. Understanding why we alter our moods helps us to identify alternative nutritional strategies to bring us into balanced self-care.

DID YOU KNOW?

When we know how an addictive substance affects our brain/mind/consciousness, we can then identify an alternative that will create a similar response but without harmful side effects if we choose to stop using it. This is the basis for the creative use of vitamins, minerals, and amino acids that we are exploring in this chapter.

Addiction-as-self-medication occurs because people choose substances to self-regulate painful feelings. They use substances—whether self-prescribed or clinician prescribed—that medicate what the brain/body cannot do for itself.

If we identify the substances that are used, we can understand what states of consciousness we seek from these substances. Then we can identify what chemical imbalances or emotional states we may be seeking to balance. We then analyze the affective and biochemical effects on the body/mind. If we understand what we are self-medicating, we can identify the nutrients that may be missing; identifying these nutrients will complement any other addiction therapy and make it more effective.

Drugs and alcohol stimulate neurotransmitter release and create a sense of pleasure and reward in the brain. But over time these exogenous chemicals suppress the ability of the brain to produce its own chemistry. The brain says, "I don't have to do much of anything; look how I am getting all this drug action without doing much at all." For example, almost all addictive substances cause an increase in dopamine, which provides feelings of reward and pleasure. But overstimulation of dopamine leads to depleted dopamine levels and, in turn, a lack of pleasure in life. This, then, drives the cycle of reaching for more dopamine-stimulating substances to get that pleasurable feeling. It is like hitting your thumb with a hammer; you feel it the first time, but if you keep hitting it, it becomes numb.

TRY THIS!

First, make a list of substances you use to self-medicate:
• What do I use to self-medicate?
• How do these substances change my mood?
• What time of day do I use these substances?
• What are the benefits or problems associated with their use?

- What brain chemicals are affected by these substances?

Next, make a list of substitutes you might make that will better serve your health and mood:
- What nutrients or supplements can be substituted for these addictive substances?
- What foods can be substituted for these addictive substances?

Alcohol

Alcohol use inhibits fat absorption and thereby impairs absorption of the omega fatty acids and vitamins A, E, and D that are normally absorbed along with dietary fats. Low levels of folate and vitamin B_{12} have been found in depressed patients who had a history of alcoholism. Binge drinking leads to insulin resistance, making individuals with a history of alcohol abuse more likely to develop type 2 diabetes and may be more vulnerable to developing dementia.

Alcohol addiction is also a physiological addiction to sugar that needs to be managed during active and long-term recovery. As people withdraw from alcohol, they often replace alcohol with refined sugar and simple carbohydrates, and increase coffee intake as part of the withdrawal and maintenance process. This can serve as a short-term transitional approach to ease withdrawal; however, it is not a long-term solution, as the sugar will exacerbate cravings.

Tobacco/Nicotine

Smoking tobacco is a form of self-medication, though in some societies, most notably American Indian, it is used in small quantities as a ritual plant. Tobacco is a euphoriant; it increases cognitive function, can appear to reduce anxiety, and possibly helps to extinguish traumatic memories. As a result, tobacco use is common among people with PTSD. Because nicotine is an antidepressant, cessation often triggers depression. Nicotine also speeds metabolism, and weight gain often follows withdrawal.

Considerable toxicity is associated with nicotine. Smokers have lower levels of B-complex, vitamin C, and the antioxidants beta-carotene, vitamin E, selenium, and zinc.

Withdrawal from nicotine generally begins within 30 minutes of smoking the last cigarette; consequent physical symptoms peak within

3 days and last for at least 4 weeks. People are subject to low energy, depression, and depressed cognitive function during the withdrawal process, so planning in advance with diet, nutrients, and exercise can mitigate those effects.

Preparation for withdrawal begins with improving diet and balancing blood sugar and oral needs by eating a mixture of high-protein foods, carbohydrates, and fats in meals every 3 to 4 hours. Choline-rich foods such as eggs, liver, and fish are very helpful.

In my clinical experience many people withdraw successfully from tobacco by substituting cannabis during the withdrawal period. The combination of the cannabis constituents and the inhalation process both likely contribute to their efficacy. THC, the psychoactive constituent, is associated with a reduction of somatic symptoms of nicotine withdrawal, suggesting the anecdotal evidence of use of cannabis during the withdrawal process has merit. Niacin supplementation is also used to treat nicotine addiction. Walking, climbing, or swimming to the point of breathing heavily helps to manage anxiety, decrease dissociation, and satisfy the urge to inhale. Heavy breathing mimics the sensation of inhaling smoke. Sweating in a sauna, steam bath, or ritual group sweat can be useful. Place ice packs on the spine between the shoulders to reduce depression and increase lung function.

Tobacco is a plant sacred to many indigenous peoples. However, its use changed over time from a ritual plant shared in a group to connect with others and the divine, to an addictive substance. Many Native peoples are currently restoring ancestral traditions in order to release the addictive tobacco in the form of cigarettes and return to traditional ways to assist in addiction recovery. There are many foods and plants like tobacco that when used in very small amounts, on an occasional basis, represent a ritual that helps families and communities cohere. Alcohol was once such a drink that over time lost its ritual and religious value and became for many a drink of addiction. Sugar cane is chewed in tropical regions as a vitamin B- and mineral-rich food that does not cause addiction, and yet over time sugar has become addictive as it lost its role as a ritual, whole food.

When considering your own food choices and addictions, explore the hidden history of these foods and return the use of these special foods, plants, and drinks to their ancestral origins as occasional rituals to be shared in a group to enhance purpose and a sense of community well-being.

FOGGY THINKING AND MEMORY LOSS

There are many nutritional problems that contribute to memory loss and cognitive decline. Risk factors for memory loss and cognitive decline include history of brain injury, chronic depression, anxiety, PTSD, poor-quality sleep, untreated sleep apnea, diabetes, and smoking. People with elevated homocysteine levels have a greater risk of cognitive decline. There is significant evidence that exposure to pesticides, herbicides, and fungicides affects cognition negatively and increases the risk of the dementia.

TRY THIS!

Eat 2 eggs daily, heart-healthy fats, and magnesium-rich foods to enhance circulation and lower blood pressure. A healthy heart leads to a healthy brain.

Dietary risk factors include foods that increase inflammation and insulin levels—such as simple carbohydrates, sugars, and trans fats—deficiency in dietary fats, and low cholesterol.

Dietary choline from eggs or from supplementation with **phosphatidylserine** and **phosphatidylcholine** is one of the most important nutritional supports for cognitive function.

TRY THIS!

Cognition Custard: Japanese Savory Steamed Egg Custard

In Japanese culture, steaming an egg custard with small pieces of chicken, shrimp, shiitake mushrooms, or gingko nuts was first done in the eighteenth century and originated in Nagasaki's Shippoku spectacular banquet cuisine. This Savory Steamed Egg Custard is adapted to the western palate and kitchen. It is elegant enough for a dinner party and simple enough to make for a quick last-minute meal. It supports cognitive function and memory. You can recreate these custards with endless variations on the ingredients added to the egg mixture.

Materials

Steamer pot or kettle with bottom water pot with a vent lid.

Mixing bowl (6 c. size)

Small mixing bowl

Cast-iron frying pan

4–6 oz. heat-resistant ramekins (ceramic steaming bowls)

Ingredients

2 oz. smoked bacon (chopped in small pieces) or smoked fish

3 oz. finely chopped onion (white or red)

4 small mushrooms (shiitake preferred, button may be used) thinly sliced

6 shrimp, medium (shelled, and tails intact)

6 large eggs

1 tbsp. wheat-free tamari

2 tbsp. toasted sesame oil

¼ c. water or chicken stock

¼ tsp. ground pepper

Sea salt, to taste

2 oz. spinach, finely chopped

2 small green onions (chopped small)

Directions

1. Heat the frying pan to medium and gently cook bacon and shelled shrimp until opaque. Remove the bacon and shrimp and place in a separate bowl, breaking the bacon up into small pieces.

2. Add the chopped onion and mushrooms to the pan and cook until translucent.

3. Add the cooked onion and mushrooms to the bacon and shrimp.

4. In the large bowl, crack six eggs and whisk to break yolks. Combine tamari, toasted sesame oil, and water or chicken stock and whisk until well mixed. Sprinkle pepper and salt to taste—not more than ¼ teaspoon.

5. Temper eggs by dropping in a few small pieces of cooked bacon and shrimp into the eggs, and then drop in the remaining heated ingredients (if using only cold smoked fish, then combine onions and mushrooms in the manner of tempering just described, and then add the remaining ingredients to the cold eggs).

6. Once all ingredients are combined, use a 4-oz. ladle and ladle the mixture into steaming cups.

7. Place cups in a steamer, bringing the steam water to a boil for about 15–20 minutes. Check if the custard has set with a wood pick or butter knife inserted into the custard—it should come out clean. Carefully remove bowls from the steamer (use gloves) and serve hot. Garnish with some fresh onion greens. Serve with small spoons.

ATTENTION-DEFICIT/HYPERACTIVITY DISORDER

Many children with a diagnosis of ADHD may be hungry, may not eat breakfast, or if they do, it may be a highly refined carbohydrate-rich breakfast. Their behaviors may reflect functional hypoglycemia and deficits of essential fatty acids. The reduction and elimination of physical exercise programs in schools and the mandatory requirement to sit for long hours, along with limits of learning style and teaching methods all contribute to behavior problems. Medications such as Adderall and Ritalin, the commonly prescribed medications, can lead to problems with sleeping, weight loss, and irritability. These medications also create functional changes in the brain, which are often then further medicated.

DID YOU KNOW?

ADHD is overdiagnosed, misdiagnosed, and often mistakenly medicated as a result. Poverty, environmental stress, violence, household stress, and developmental trauma all contribute to learning and attention problems and may be mistaken for ADHD. Attention and focus can be supported with good food and nutrients.

Children with a diagnosis of ADHD often have low levels of zinc and iron, both of which are required for neurotransmitter synthesis. Dopamine and essential fatty acid levels may be low as well. Food sensitivities, a highly refined carbohydrate diet, food coloring, microbiome imbalance, and toxic exposures—such as heavy metals and environmental toxins—are also common in people with symptoms of ADHD; some children and adults are also sensitive to foods containing salicylates.

TRY THIS!

Focus Smoothie

Instead of asking children and teens to swallow a bunch of capsules, make this smoothie for breakfast or an afternoon snack. The egg provides choline for focus and memory. If you can obtain pasture-raised local eggs, those are the very best, and you may use them in raw form. Otherwise do a 2-minute soft boil, cool the egg and then add it to the smoothie.

Ingredients

1 c. almond or hemp milk

2 tbsp. raw almond butter

½ tsp. of hemp, oil

1 frozen banana

1–2 tbsp. raw organic cacao powder (no sugar)

Free amino acids (powder) containing tryptophan or 5-HTP

Probiotic powder

Optional:

Vitamin/mineral complex powder (copper free/iron free)

5–10 drops stevia (sweeten to taste)

Place ingredients in the blender in the order listed, blending as you add. Makes 1–2 servings.

PAIN AND FIBROMYALGIA

Chronic pain commonly co-occurs with PTSD, depression, and substance abuse. It also contributes to insomnia. Fibromyalgia is a sleep/pain syndrome that co-occurs at high rates with a history of early childhood trauma that disrupts body function.

Foods that are anti-inflammatory, analgesic nutrients and herbs, and water-based movement and massage—such as Watsu—combine to provide a protocol that will reduce pain.

TRY THIS!

Pain-Free Smoothie

A diet rich in healthy fats, green and red/purple foods (no sugar, grains, or nightshades), proteolytic enzymes morning and evening on an empty stomach, and this smoothie provide a solid start to reducing pain and inflammation. This smoothie contains a nutrient/herbal blend that reduces the inflammatory responses in the body.

Drink this once a day, varying the type of berries:

1 c. hemp, coconut, or almond milk

1 c. fresh or frozen blueberries

½ tsp. fish oil

½ tsp. evening primrose oil

Free amino acid powder with tryptophan or 5-HTP

DL-phenylalanine powder (500 mg)

Probiotic powder

KappArest ™ NF-kappaB targeting powder: contains turmeric, boswellia, propolis, green tea, ginger, rosemary, resveratrol, alpha lipoic acid.

Directions

Add all the liquids and fruit together and blend, then add the powders one at a time and blend.

NEXT STEPS

- Identify the nutritional factors that may contribute to mental health problems.
- Make a list of substances that you are addicted to and the alternatives you can substitute.
- Identify heart-healthy behaviors that will enhance brain and cognitive function.
- Identify at least 1 or 2 recipes you want to try, and engage friends and family members in making and tasting them together.
- Purchase your 3 most important nutrients for your brain/mind health.

CHAPTER 8

The Right Foods for You: Adapt Your Diet for Allergies and Sensitivities

We make food choices for many reasons: family experience, religious and cultural belief systems, and the sense of taste and satisfaction. We also make choices or feel driven to eat certain foods due to allergies and sensitivities. What you choose to eat can be a response to cravings and the effects of food chemicals on the brain and mood.

Mental and physical reactions to foods and to food additives can go undetected for many years, but if you eliminate certain foods, it is likely to lead to improved well-being. Symptoms can improve, and frequently adverse reactions will resolve.

If you suspect you may have food allergies or sensitivities, I suggest the following four-step process for finding the sensitivity-savvy diet that best suits the unique needs of your body and mind:

- **Step 1:** Identify the diet that makes you feel best.
- **Step 2:** Choose a special simplified diet to help jumpstart the first days and weeks of your dietary recovery.
- **Step 3:** Identify your particular food allergies and sensitivities.
- **Step 4:** Make a plan for short- and long-term change.

STEP 1: IDENTIFY THE DIET THAT MAKES YOU FEEL BEST

The first step to identifying an appropriate diet is to further explore your nutritional type (carnivore, balanced/mixed, or vegetarian) and the ideal range of food types and ratios that will benefit you. Remember your metabolizer type? Refer to the table below to help you match your nutritional metabolism to the ideal food ratios.

Nutritional Types and Best Foods			
Type	Metabolism	Blood pH	Best foods
Fast metabolizer	Burns carbohydrates fast	Acidic	Carnivore and purines (organ meats, sardines, etc.)
Slow metabolizer	Burns carbohydrates more slowly	Alkaline	Vegetarian (lacto-ovo w/ less animal products)
Mixed metabolizer	Burns balanced	Balanced	Mixed animal and plant proteins/carbs

STEP 2: CHOOSE A SPECIAL SIMPLIFIED DIET TO HELP JUMPSTART THE FIRST DAYS AND WEEKS OF YOUR DIETARY RECOVERY.

Decide if you will benefit from any special type of diet for the short term to jumpstart your recovery.

There are nearly as many different diets as there are people. Diet names come and go. But the basics of all diets are the same—the ratios of proteins, fats, and carbohydrates and the effects they purport to achieve. The best approach for following a food system is to find one that feels "right" in the gut. Dietary needs shift over time depending upon age, activity level, or illness, so it's important to be open to making changes as your body's needs change. Let's remember our savvy diet principle: There is no one right diet for everyone. The question you should ask: Is this diet right for me?

I often suggest the anti-inflammatory diet, a 2–3 day vegetable juice fast, or a mono diet for this phase, but you might also consider one of the other diets described below. These diets provide a spectrum of approaches to address biochemical individuality. The key is to simplify food choices and focus on using these options for days or even weeks to explore how you feel. Options including removing foods that are likely to cause negative reactions. They include carnivore diets as well as balanced/mixed and vegetarian types of diets—a whole range of tasty options!

Cleansing and Anti-Inflammatory Diets

The benefits of specific diets result both from what you eat and also what you don't eat. The following cleansing and anti-inflammatory diets provide a structured approach to eliminating foods that can contribute to mental health symptoms.

Anti-Inflammatory Diet

This diet is an excellent first step to change your diet. It may be used for 2–4 weeks at a time. It is helpful for people with pain and depression. If it feels too restrictive, some of the inflammatory foods can be eliminated one at a time while beneficial foods are added. The diet is higher in carbohydrates than some people need, so that people can still gain benefits by eliminating the inflammatory foods such as wheat, corn, soy, dairy, nightshade vegetables, sugar, margarine, partially hydrogenated oils, alcohol, and peanuts.

The anti-inflammatory diet is designed to reduce the intake of inflammatory foods. It emphasizes eating a variety of fresh fruits and vegetables while eliminating the intake of processed and fast foods. The diet consists of 40%–50% carbohydrates, 30% fat, and 20%–30% protein. Carbohydrates include low-glycemic foods such as brown rice, beans, sweet potatoes, and winter squash. Animal proteins from fish, natural cheese, and yogurt are emphasized, as well as vegetable protein.

Other aspects of the diet include drinking tea instead of coffee, drinking red wine instead of other alcohols, and eating dark (sugarless) chocolate in moderation.

Over time you will need to add in saturated fats like raw butter, and people who are more naturally carnivore will benefit from adding more animal-based proteins.

Gut and Psychology Syndrome (GAPS) Diet

This diet was developed to treat children (and adults) with the autism spectrum disorders, ADD/ADHD, dyspraxia, dyslexia, and schizophrenia in particular, but it can be beneficial to anyone who is reactive to dairy and gluten. It focuses on reducing inflammation of the gut walls to reduce permeability and entry of toxins into the bloodstream. There are three main principles of the GAPS diet: (1) healing the gut, (2) restoring beneficial bacteria to the gut, and (3) detoxification. This diet is safe and effective for all mental health disorders.

Fasting and Detoxification Diets

Fasting is the voluntary act of abstaining from food and/or liquid for a given amount of time for health-related, spiritual, or political reasons. Fasts may include the consumption of only liquids. Mono diets may be used for detoxification.

Fasting for 1–3 days can have positive effects, such as increasing immune health, disease prevention, mental clarity, and improving digestive health. Fasting gives the digestive system a break and allows toxins to be eliminated. The energy that is normally used for digestion can be used for healing and repairing damaged tissues. Many benefits can be obtained from juice or vegetable fasts, which include only fruit and vegetable juices and water, but no solid foods. Juice or vegetable fasts provide concentrated nutrients and can be used for short periods of 1–3 days for detoxification. Water fasts eliminate all food and liquids other than water from the diet. They are generally ill advised for mental or physical health.

Fruit and vegetable fasts restrict all foods except fruits and vegetables— which are high in nutrients—and allow digestion to rest and detoxification to occur. Mono diets are fasts in which only one food is consumed for a given period of time to give the digestive system a rest while supplying necessary nutrition—such as a rice fast or a diet of only one type of vegetable.

Side effects of fasting include headaches, nausea, foul body odor, bad breath, and intense hunger. Nutrient deficiencies can be a problem if fasts are done for long periods of time. Other possible side effects are constipation, dizziness, fatigue, dehydration, and gallstones. Fasting is contraindicated during pregnancy and nursing, and for those with diabetes, heart disease, cancer, elevated fevers, and those on medication. Starvation may be induced by strict fasting, which could lead to electrolyte imbalances, renal failure, cardiac arrhythmias, and even death. People with anorexia nervosa should not fast. It is important to transition slowly into the fast and out of the fast. Limit any fast to 2–3 days. Do not use water-only fasts.

If you want to explore fasting, choose intermittent fasting. Take one day a week when you give your digestion a rest by drinking only fresh vegetable juices with water and clear broths. Or you can fast for 12–16 hours: Eat the last meal at 8:00 p.m. and drink only water until 12:00 noon the next day. Just as we sleep to rest, so does the digestive system benefit from a rest.

Caution: If you experience reactive hypoglycemia (habitual low energy up to 4 hours after a meal), fasting is not right for you. Spend several months restoring your blood glucose handling before embarking on fasting.

TRY THIS!

Khichdi Fast

Khichdi is an Indian dish that is easily digested and can be used after a period of intemperance or to eliminate allergens from the diet. It can also be used to transition into and out of other more extreme liquid fasts, as a recovery diet after surgery or other illnesses, or during times of emotional stress when digestion is taxed. The spices in this dish are soothing and aid elimination and detoxification.

Ingredients

1 c. split yellow mung dahl beans (available at Asian or Indian grocery stores; do not use whole mung beans—which are green—or yellow split peas)

¼–½ c. long grain white rice or white basmati rice

1 tsp. each: black mustard seeds, cumin, and turmeric powder

½ tsp. each: coriander powder, fennel seeds, and fenugreek seeds

3 cloves

7–10 c. water

3 bay leaves

1 tbsp. fresh ginger root, grated

½ tsp. sea salt

½ c. chopped fresh cilantro leaves

Directions

1. Wash split yellow mung beans and rice together until water runs clear.
2. In a pre-heated large pot, dry roast all the spices (except the bay leaves and ginger) on medium heat for a few minutes, stirring and making sure not to burn.

3. Add dahl and rice and stir, coating the rice and beans with the spices.

4. Add water and bay leaves and bring to a boil. Boil for 10 minutes.

5. Turn heat to low, add the ginger, cover the pot, and continue to cook until dahl and rice become soft (about 40 minutes).

6. The chopped cilantro can be added just before serving. Add salt to taste.

Carnivore Diets

Carnivore diets emphasize animal proteins and fats and are ideal for fast metabolizers and others who require higher levels of foods with purines and other acid forming foods. A carnivore diet is also suitable for some people short-term in order to withdraw from refined carbohydrate addiction and cravings. These diets can be adjusted by balancing the percentages of protein and fats with vegetables and fruits.

The Basic Carnivore Diet

Sometimes called the paleo, cave-person, or Atkins diet, this is a low-carbohydrate diet. This diet is very effective to eliminate carbohydrate cravings. By lowering carbohydrate consumption, the body switches from using glucose for energy to using stored body fat in a process called *ketosis*. Proteins and healthy fats are increased in the diet. Carbohydrates—like fruits, starchy vegetables, grains, breakfast cereals, flour, and sugars—are restricted. On this diet it is possible to become deficient in vitamins B5, C, D, E, and K. Fiber, selenium, potassium, magnesium, and B-complex vitamins and minerals should be supplemented. The difference between the paleo and Atkins diets is that the paleo diet does not include dairy.

The diet includes grass-fed meats, fish and seafood, nuts and seeds, vegetables, fruits, roots, eggs, and healthy oils, while excluding dairy, carbohydrates like potatoes and refined flour and sugar, grains, legumes, refined salt, and refined vegetable oils. It is high in protein, fat, fiber, and nutrients, and low in carbohydrates and sodium. The diet is a superior diet for hypoglycemia and diabetes and is a beneficial diet for mental illness, including depression, anxiety, and psychotic disorders. It is important to ensure sufficient fiber in vegetables and fruits, and to include calcium and vitamins.

People who are eliminating carbohydrate addiction can be successful with this diet for short term use (1–4 weeks).

Carnivore with Dairy and Grains

This diet is similar to the paleo diet, but it allows dairy and/or grains for people who are not sensitive to lactose or casein, or to gluten or non-gluten grains. Sheep or goat dairy is preferred. This diet is also recommended for withdrawing from alcohol and sugar addiction. The diet is an excellent transitional diet to get off fast food, allowing for animal proteins and fats that are satisfying. I recommend this diet to individuals who eat a lot of fast food or poor-quality protein and fats. I ask them to substitute free-range organic beef, pork, eggs, and good-quality raw cheeses for the fast-food meats and fats they are used to. Lettuce wraps make a great substitute for sandwiches, as you detoxify from fast foods.

The Balanced or Mixed Oxidizer Diet

This diet is for people who do well eating almost any good-quality food. It emphasizes lots of plant-based foods, both raw and cooked, and whole grains, legumes, healthy fats like butter, sesame oil, and olive oil, and allows for fish, poultry, and beef, lamb and pork 3–4 times a week, as well as plenty of fresh fruit. Raw nuts and seeds are also an important part of the diet.

Vegetarian Diets

While there is a wide range of vegetarian diets, from vegan (no animal products) to lacto-ovo (includes dairy and eggs) vegetarian, the basic vegetarian diet excludes meat of any kind, including seafood, poultry, and red meat. One of the primary reasons people choose a vegetarian diet is due to the belief that it is unethical to kill animals for food. This diet is also chosen for health, religious, economic, environmental, political, or personal reasons.

Lacto vegetarians eat dairy but not eggs. Semivegetarian diets are primarily vegetarian but may include some animal flesh, such as pescatarianism in which seafood is the only meat consumed, or a pollotarian diet in which poultry is allowed. Macrobiotic diets include whole grains and legumes, and they may also include some seafood. Semivegetarian diets are sometimes used when transitioning into or out of a completely vegetarian diet, or for other reasons such as dislike for certain types of meat or to simply reduce meat consumption.

Animal protein is low in a vegetarian diet, but lacto-ovo vegetarians who consume animal by-products, such as cheese, milk, and eggs, are usually able to consume enough protein and the necessary amino acids. A vegetarian diet can provide adequate protein, but it is important to eat a wide variety of foods and proteins to ensure proper nutrition. Vitamin B_{12} deficiency is a risk for vegetarians, as this vitamin comes only from animal protein and thus should be supplemented.

A deficiency of dietary sulfur can occur in those following a strict vegetarian or vegan diet, as they are not consuming the dietary protein that provides the sulfur-containing amino acids. This deficiency can lead to problems with protein and enzyme activity in the body, as well as to problems with bones, joints, metabolism, and connective tissues. Sulfur is important for the proper functioning of insulin, detoxification, carbohydrate metabolism, electron transport, and the synthesis of metabolic intermediates like glutathione.

Vegetarians may be susceptible to subclinical protein malnutrition that can lead to an increased risk of cardiovascular diseases. You can avoid this by including a broad base of plant proteins that deliver the full complement of amino acids, such as lysine-rich pumpkin seeds and pistachio nuts. Make sure to include plenty of saturated fat sources. Supplements should include vitamin B complex, the essential 1,000–2,000 mg daily of vitamin B_{12} (methycobalamin), and a minerals complex with a balance of calcium and magnesium. Iodine is an essential supplement; generous use of sea vegetables may be sufficient, but iodine should be supplemented if dairy use is low—iodized salt can help. Vitamin D intake should average about 2,000 IU a day depending on geographical location (how much sunlight you receive). Although it is important for everyone, vegetarians especially should obtain a Tissue Mineral Analysis (hair test) yearly, as well as a blood test, to assess and ensure adequate levels and ratios of vitamins and minerals See the Resources section for where to obtain these tests.

STEP 3: IDENTIFY FOOD ALLERGIES AND SENSITIVITIES

The next step is to discover what foods you may be allergic or sensitive to. There are also additives and preservatives that almost everyone is sensitive to and are worth eliminating. Sometimes eliminating certain foods may be the easiest first step.

As a basic first step, I encourage people to eliminate all packaged foods that have additives and preservatives, regardless of whether they are sensitive to them, and to choose fresh whole foods instead.

Food allergies and sensitivities are common in people who experience poor mental health. Inflammatory reactions caused by diet fall into two categories: food allergies and food sensitivities. Some of the more common food allergies that affect mental health are glutinous grains and dairy products, but food allergies are not limited to these major categories. There are also food-induced autoimmune diseases, including multiple sclerosis, rheumatoid arthritis, celiac and inflammatory bowel disease, type 1 diabetes, autoimmune thyroid disease, Sjögren's syndrome, psoriasis. Food-based autoimmune reactions have also been implicated in schizophrenia and autism spectrum disorder.

How Food Allergies Work

Food allergies involve reactivity of the immune system. Allergies are often genetic and hereditary. Allergies can be present in childhood through adulthood and are more likely if a parent has an allergy. They can also develop in response to foods that are eaten often. Allergies can develop in adulthood and may be linked to chronic stress that disrupts immune function. Allergies can also develop as a result of chronic infections, eating poor-quality or pro-inflammatory foods, toxic exposure, nutritional deficits, and chronic stress.

Symptoms of food allergy can occur immediately after ingesting the food or up to several hours later. Symptoms may be mild or severe. Mild symptoms of food allergy include itching in the nose, mouth, eyes, and throat; hives; or gastrointestinal problems like vomiting and diarrhea. More severe reactions include angioedema or anaphylaxis.

Allergens

While common allergens include milk, eggs, wheat, soy, tree nuts, peanuts, fish, strawberries, and shellfish, nearly any food can cause an allergic reaction. Pollen-food allergy syndrome—also known as *oral allergy syndrome* (OAS—occurs when certain vegetables, fruits, nuts, or other foods cause an allergic reaction in people who have hay fever due to a similarity in the proteins in the pollens and the foods. For example, a ragweed allergy can cause a food allergy to bananas, tomatoes, or melons. Cooking food usually prevents this cross-reactivity from occurring.

Food allergies can be tested by a skin prick test, blood test, oral food challenge, the pulse test, or elimination diets. The best approach to treatment is elimination of the allergen.

THE PULSE TEST

One way to begin to test for food allergy or sensitivity is the pulse test, a simple, do-it-yourself method for determining negative reactions to foods. It is not recommended in cases of severe allergic reactions like anaphylaxis.

Pulse Test Directions
- Begin the day by taking your pulse before you get out of bed. Count your pulse beats for 1 minute and record them.
- Take your pulse 1 minute before each meal.
- Take your pulse 30 minutes after each meal, then again in another 30 minutes, and a third time 30 minutes after that.
- Take your pulse just before going to bed.
- Record each pulse that you take along with the foods eaten at each meal.
- Continue the pulse-taking and recording of meals eaten for 2–3 days.
- Take note of meals that caused pulse increases of more than 6 to 8 beats per minute, and identify foods within those meals that could be the cause.
- Foods that are suspected of causing pulse increases can then be tested individually. Take your pulse before eating the suspected food item and again 30 minutes afterward.

Eliminate from your diet foods that cause pulse increases of more than 6 to 8 beats per minute.

Food Sensitivity and Intolerance

Food sensitivities are the most common type of diet-induced inflammatory reaction. These sensitivities contribute to poor mental health and yet may be disguised in their presentation. Thus, it may take many years to realize that food sensitivities can be a cause or contributing factor to any diagnosis or symptom.

It can be difficult to identify trigger foods inasmuch as the symptoms may not manifest directly after you consume the offending food, and the amount of food eaten can greatly affect the presentation of symptoms.

Symptoms of food intolerances vary widely and can manifest quickly after eating the food or may require up to several days to appear. Sometimes the skin shows signs of food intolerance, like eczema, acne dermatitis, rashes, or hives. The digestive system can be affected with symptoms such as gas, bloating, cramping, diarrhea, constipation, irritable bowel syndrome, nausea, and ulcers in the mouth. The respiratory tract can also be affected.

There are many mental health and physical conditions that may be related to food and food-chemical sensitivities, such as fibromyalgia, GERD, inflammatory bowel syndrome, obesity, migraines, ADHD, autism spectrum disorders, depression, insomnia, and chronic fatigue syndrome.

Food intolerances and sensitivities can also have a psychological component when foods are associated with traumatizing events in state-dependent learning memory and behavior. This occurs when an offending food is associated with a negative event in one's life and the body associates the pain of the event and the symptoms with the food or even the time of year the event occurred. This can make teasing out cause and effect very challenging. Then the symptoms can become conditioned and no longer require the food or environmental trigger; they just continue.

Elimination Diets

The elimination diet is an effective and safe way to assess and treat food intolerances. Eliminating a food or food group for 3 or 4 weeks while monitoring symptoms allows sufficient time to observe symptom changes. If symptoms improve during this time, the food is reintroduced to see if it causes the symptoms to worsen. If symptoms improve when the food is eliminated and return when the food is reintroduced, the food should be excluded from the diet for at least 6 months. Strict adherence to the diet is necessary for accuracy and to ensure sufficient time for inflammation caused by the food to heal. Once an offending food is identified, it may be possible to eat it once in a while without symptoms, but only on special occasions, and this must be assessed individually.

Guide to Foods on the Elimination Diet	
Foods to include in the diet	Foods to eliminate from the diet
Coconut oil, cold-pressed olive oil, flaxseed oil	Alcohol, caffeine (coffee, black tea, green tea, yerba mate, soda), chocolate
Fish, lamb, turkey, wild game	Beans (all beans—soybeans, tofu, tempeh, peas, lentils)
Fresh water, herbal teas, rice or coconut milk—unsweetened	Citrus fruits
Fruits (fresh)	Condiments (ketchup, mayonnaise, mustard, soy sauce, vinegar, relish, chutney, barbeque sauce)
Sea salt, herbs and spices	Corn
Rice, buckwheat	Dairy
Stevia	Eggs
Vegetables (raw, steamed, sautéed, or roasted), sweet potatoes or yams	Gluten—wheat, barley, spelt, kamut, rye, oats (unless gluten-free)
	Hydrogenated oils, margarine
	Meats (beef, chicken, pork, cold cuts, bacon, hot dogs, sausage, canned meats), meat substitutes (made from soy or gluten), shellfish and canned fish products
	Nightshade vegetables (tomatoes, eggplant, potatoes, bell peppers, chili peppers, paprika)
	Nuts, seeds
	Sweeteners (honey, sugar, maple syrup, corn syrup)

After 3 weeks on the elimination diet, you reintroduce one food at a time for 1 day. For example, if you decide to end the elimination diet by reintroducing corn, you would add corn or a corn product to a couple of meals for 1 day. Then for the next 2 days you would not eat corn, but you would monitor to see if any reactions occur. If not, you can continue to eat corn, and after those 2 days you can add another food back into your diet and follow the same process of 1 day with the new food and 2 days without while monitoring for symptoms. The elimination diet and reintroduction phase should take about 5–6 weeks total.

Among the first foods to start eliminating are grains containing gluten (wheat, bulgur, barley, rye, couscous, kamut, semolina, spelt, triticale, and oats), cow's milk (milk and cheese products), and soy—but any food or food group (salicylates, nightshades, additives) that can cause reactions can be eliminated.

Common Food Allergies and Sensitivities

The following foods are among those that cause the most problems in people, along with some delicious, satisfying recipes.

Lactose

Lactose is a sugar that is present in dairy products. A deficiency in the enzyme that digests lactose leads to intolerance. This is very common. For example, African natives and peoples from Asia have the highest rates of intolerance (80%–100%), followed by African Americans and Mexican natives (70%–80%), Mediterranean and those of Jewish descent (60%–90%), and Northern Europeans (1%–5%).

Some people are able to handle small amounts of lactose without triggering a reaction. Some people with lactose intolerance may be able to tolerate dairy products that have a higher fat content, such as pure cream or butter, since the lactose content is lower in these products.

Many processed foods contain lactose, so it is important to read food labels and check for milk, lactose, whey, curds, dry milk solids, nonfat dry milk powder, and milk by-products. As a general rule, I discourage all children and adults from drinking cow's milk or eating cow's cheese.

Casein

Casein is a protein found in milk and milk products. Products with higher protein content, such as yogurt, cheese, kefir, milk, and ice cream, tend to be higher in casein. Butter and cream contain only small amounts of casein. Casein is often added to nondairy cheeses to give them the melting quality of real cheese.

Casein sensitivity has been implicated in schizophrenia, depression, and the autism spectrum disorders. Casein is the major ingredient in the anxiolytics that have the generic term lactium or brand name De-Stress™. However, this is a specially prepared peptide derived from casein and does not appear to contribute to allergic or sensitive reactions.

Gluten

The easiest way to withdraw from gluten is to follow a 7-day high-fat and high-protein diet. Generally, the physiological craving for gluten and carbohydrates diminishes significantly after 7 days, but the diet can be continued for longer if necessary. A modification of this diet involves incorporating root vegetables such as sweet potatoes, yuca (manioc or cassava), parsnips, carrots, and squash. These foods satisfy the need for fiber and for something sweet. Unlike other sweets, they raise the blood sugar level slowly and they contain nourishing vitamins and minerals. Sometimes people who are addicted to carbohydrates like the sensation of fullness that these foods bring. This can be produced with root vegetables by taking some fiber in a drink—for example, a gluten-free source such as psyllium.

There are many gluten-free carbohydrate substitutes such as the following milled flours: rice, potato, coconut, almond, buckwheat, sorghum, sweet potato, bean/cassava/rice mixtures, and tapioca. Gluten sensitivity may also be tied to glucose dysregulation and thus mood swings. It takes 3 months, in general, for the intestinal inflammation associated with gluten sensitivity to heal. However, changes in mood, a reduction in joint stiffness, and the lifting of depression will be apparent sooner. In severe cases of sensitivity, it is always wise to eliminate all gluten products. In mild cases of carbohydrate addiction, it is possible to reintegrate the use of carbohydrates with gluten on some special occasions without adverse effects. However, as in the case of alcohol addiction, some people do better with total abstinence while others appear to manage limited quantities. Since glutinous carbohydrates are often used as comfort foods, you could apply the principle of substituting a less addictive substance like a stevia-sweetened cocoa with cream for a glutinous carbohydrate.

TRY THIS!

Gluten-Free and Casein-Free Pancakes Topped With Fruit Sauce

Children and adults alike love pancakes, but ordinarily they contain poor-quality flours and sugars. However, the pancakes in this recipe are ideal for everyone. They are light and fluffy, sweet and satisfying, and make a wonderful Sunday morning meal. Place one or two poached eggs on the side with some organic bacon or sausage for an anti-hypoglycemic meal.

Dry Ingredients

1¾ c. rice flour

¼ c. buckwheat flour

¼ c. almond flour

1 tbsp. chia seeds (for fiber)

1½ tsp. baking powder

¼ c. tapioca flour

Pinch of sea salt

Wet Ingredients

1 c. almond milk or coconut milk

1 c. water (or as needed)

1 tbsp. vinegar

2 eggs, beaten

4 tbsp. coconut oil, melted

4 drops of liquid stevia

1 tsp. vanilla extract

Sauce Ingredients

1 c. defrosted organic berries or other fruits like mango or pineapple chopped

1 tbsp. organic butter

1–4 drops stevia liquid, to taste

Serving Suggestions

Top pancakes with butter, fresh berries, almond butter, yogurt, and/or nuts.

Directions

1. Whisk together the dry ingredients in a large mixing bowl. In a separate bowl, whisk together the wet ingredients. Add the wet ingredients to the dry ingredients and mix until almost smooth. The consistency should be pourable; if it is too thick, add a little more water or milk. Let sit for about 10 minutes to blend and hydrate the chia seeds. It should show signs of little gas bubbles due to the vinegar/baking powder reaction.

2. Lightly grease your pan or griddle with coconut oil and heat over medium-high heat.

3. When the pan is hot, use a ladle to pour the pancake batter into the pan. (Turn heat down a bit if the first cakes are a bit scorched.)

4. Wait until you see bubbles forming in the pancake and the edges look cooked, then flip the pancake with a spatula. Cook for another minute or two until firm, then serve. Repeat with the rest of the batter.

Making the Sauce

1. Defrost frozen berries or other fruits like mango and pineapple and lightly heat in a pan with added butter and stevia. Bring to a near boil, simmer for a few minutes, and decant into a syrup bowl with a spoon.
2. Pour over the top of the pancakes.

Tip: Pancakes are best when eaten immediately, but if you need to keep the pancakes warm, use a large, shallow serving bowl and place a towel inside it. Wrap the pancakes in the towel. This will keep them warm and prevent them from drying out.

Always read the label. The key to understanding the gluten-free diet and the additive-free diet is to become a good ingredient-label reader. Gluten is everywhere now and even used as an additive, so there is a lot of hidden gluten in prepared and packaged foods. Just because it is not listed does not mean it is not there. There are many gluten-free foods and bread/grain substitutes. Choose from many fresh, healthy foods like fruits, vegetables, beans, dairy, nuts and nut flours, sweet potatoes, buckwheat, amaranth, potato flour, and gluten-free grains like sorghum, quinoa, or rice. Millet along with quinoa is highly nutritious, versatile, and easy to prepare. The best options are the natural flours made with nuts and seeds, and flours made from coconut, almond, rice, potato, and tapioca.

TRY THIS!

Curried Quinoa

Quinoa is a seed and is a perfect substitute for a grain dish. It is one of the oldest foods in the western hemisphere and is a complete protein source. Quinoa is failsafe; it can be made as a thick porridge or fluffy like rice. It's a perfect substitute for coming off of gluten and grains in general.

Ingredients

1½ c. water

¾ c. quinoa

2 tbsp. coconut oil

½ c. coarsely chopped sweet onion

¼ c. red bell peppers, chopped

½ c. frozen peas

¾ c. chopped Fuji apple

½ c. pecans, coarsely chopped

1 tbsp. freshly grated ginger

1 tbsp. curry powder

¼ tsp. salt

Directions

1. Begin by rinsing thoroughly in water and then draining the quinoa. Then bring the water to a boil. Add the quinoa, reduce the heat to a low simmer, cover and cook for 15–20 minutes.
2. While the quinoa is cooking, heat the coconut oil in a medium skillet and sauté the onions on low until lightly browned.
3. Add the chopped bell peppers and cook for two minutes.
4. Add the peas, apple, pecans, and ginger to the pan and cook for another 2 minutes.
5. When the quinoa is finished cooking, add to the onion mixture. Add the curry and salt, and stir to combine.

TRY THIS!

Millet

Millet is one of my favorite grains. It is easy to prepare, mild in taste, and can be eaten with some sweet dried fruit for breakfast or as a snack, or with a touch of melted goat cheddar for dinner. It is nourishing and sticks to the belly. Like cruciferous foods, millet can suppress thyroid function if eaten in excess, so integrate it gently into your grain repertoire.

Ingredients

1 c. raw millet

2 c. water (or broth)

¼ tsp. salt, optional

1 tbsp. unsalted butter or coconut oil

Directions

1. In a large, dry saucepan, toast the raw millet over medium heat for 4–5 minutes or until it turns a rich golden brown and the grains become fragrant. Do not burn.
2. Add the water and salt to the pan and stir. Bring to a boil; then turn the heat to

low. Add the butter and cover the pot. Simmer until the grains absorb most of the water, about 15 minutes.

3. Remove from the heat and allow it to sit, covered and removed from heat, for 10 minutes.

4. Fluff the millet with a fork and add additional salt, if desired. Millet does not keep well and is best served warm.

Variations

To make millet porridge, increase the liquid to 3 cups and stir every few minutes as the millet simmers.

Corn

Corn is one of the more challenging food allergies to manage, since corn is so prevalent in foods produced in the United States. From cornstarch and corn syrup to ingredients like dextrose, it can be very difficult to find packaged foods that do not contain some form of corn. That doesn't mean that there isn't a whole world of delicious foods too if you have a corn sensitivity! It just means that it's more crucial than ever to *always read the label*. Avoiding packaged foods altogether is the best approach.

Nightshades

Nightshade foods are members of a large plant family that includes tomatoes, potatoes (excluding sweet potatoes and yams), eggplant, and peppers (excluding black pepper). Symptoms of nightshade sensitivity include muscle pain and tightness, arthritis, sensitivity to weather changes, morning stiffness, slow healing, gallbladder problems, heartburn, and GERD.

To test for nightshade sensitivity, begin by conducting a self-inventory of pain and swelling of joints. Rate how you feel on a scale of 1 to 10, with 10 being terrible joint pain with stiffness. Eliminate all nightshade foods during 4 weeks, and at the end of the period conduct another self-inventory. If you are sensitive to nightshades, you will feel better after 4 weeks without them. You can test this by returning to the use of nightshades for 1–2 weeks and observe that the pain and stiffness will return. Some people can sharply reduce their intake of nightshades and still tolerate them on occasion. If you enjoy barbecue sauce, use the recipe below and modify it to avoid nightshades.

Papaya Barbeque Sauce

This is an exotic and healthy alternative to traditional barbeque sauce. If you want to make an anti-inflammatory, nightshade-free version, just leave out the crushed red chili pepper.

Ingredients

1 tbsp. organic extra-virgin coconut oil

1 medium onion, chopped

2 cloves garlic, minced

1 tsp. crushed red chili pepper

½ tsp. cumin powder

1 tsp. oregano

1 c. dark brown sugar

5 drops of stevia liquid

1 lime (zest and juice)

½ c. apple cider vinegar, to taste

2 lb. ripe papaya, diced

½ tsp. sea salt

3–4 drops liquid smoke

Directions

1. Cook and stir onions and garlic in oil until onions are translucent. Add the chilies, cumin, and oregano.
2. Add sugar, stevia, lime, and apple cider vinegar. Bring to a boil.
3. Add papaya and salt. Return to a boil and simmer 15 minutes.
4. Add the liquid smoke.
5. Remove mixture from the heat and allow it to cool. Puree in a blender until smooth.

Other Allergy-Inducing Substances		
Name	Adverse reactions	Food sources
Histamine	Anxiety, headaches, migraines, mood swings, itchiness, hives, and asthma. High levels of systemic histamine are associated with OCD, oppositional defiant disorder, and seasonal affective disorder.	Fermented foods like red wine, aged cheese, and sauerkraut; leftovers or overripe foods; cultured, processed, smoked, and fermented meats; citrus fruits; tea; chocolate; and alcohol.

Salicylates	Anxiety and depression; ADHD; asthma and breathing problems; headaches; nasal congestion; itching, skin rash, or hives; swelling of the hands, feet, and face; and stomach pain. Found in people with multiple-chemical sensitivity.	Tea, coffee, dried herbs and spices, black pepper, Granny Smith apples, cherries, strawberries, dried fruit, tomatoes, fruit juices, cider, wine, peppermint, and licorice.
Sulfites (includes sulfur dioxide, potassium bisulfite, potassium metabisulfite, sodium bisulfite, sodium metabisulfite, and sodium sulfite)	Asthma, wheezing, hives, itchiness, vomiting, upset stomach, diarrhea.	Wine (especially non-organic white and sweet wine), dried fruits, frozen shrimp, some beverages and medications.

Common Chemical Sensitivities

Reactions to chemicals in food or the environment may be immediate or delayed, and thus are challenging to identify. There is no benefit to these chemicals, so it is wise to avoid foods that contain them.

Neurotoxins

Neurotoxins and excitotoxins are substances added to foods that prevent nerves from functioning normally by interfering with their electrical activities. They are found in most packaged foods and include ingredients like dough conditioners; seasonings; yeast extract; carrageenan; maltodextrin; hydrolyzed vegetable protein; sodium fluoride; sodium caseinate; calcium caseinate; chicken, pork, or beef flavoring; disodium anything; smoke flavoring and anything called *autolyzed*; whey protein concentrate; natural flavors or spices; and additives such as glutamate and aspartate.

Avoid monosodium glutamate, natural flavors, aspartame, sucralose, hydrolyzed vegetable protein, and all carbonated soft drinks.

> ## TRY THIS!
>
> **Detoxification With Water**
>
> Water is essential for flushing out toxins, so it's important to know your individual needs for water.
>
> **Calculate Your Requirements for Water**
>
> We are made up of water. Think of a big balloon filled with water and a big fat globule called the brain at the top. That's our body. Dehydration contributes to fatigue, depression, and toxicity. I often suggest to my clients that they fill water glasses and place them in every room they visit during the day so they will drink their requisite daily fluid. (Coffee and black teas do not count toward the total, but herbal tea and broths do.) As a general rule, we need to drink 30%–50% of our body weight in ounces of water daily. Calculate your body weight in pounds and divide it in half. This will be the number of ounces of water you need to drink daily. For example, if you weigh 150 pounds, drink 75 ounces of water daily.

Everyone—that means you, too—will benefit from eliminating soft drinks, including diet sodas. This should be one of the first three action items in everyone's plan to improve their mental health. The following recipe for a raspberry lime rickey is adapted from a drink that originated in New England during the Prohibition era when people sought satisfying substitutes for alcohol.

Raspberry Lime Rickey

Ingredients

Crushed ice

Juice from 1 lime

½ c. frozen raspberries

1 glass of sparkling mineral water

1 to 5 drops liquid stevia, to taste

Directions

Fill glass with ice. Add lime juice, raspberries, sparkling water, and stevia; stir to combine.

Heavy Metals

Heavy metals are a well-established cause of mental illness, in particular learning disorders (associated with lead and molybdenum) and cognitive decline (associated with arsenic, mercury, aluminum, and lead).

DID YOU KNOW?

Seaweed and Coriander

Seaweeds are a significant detoxifying food source (particularly kelp with its natural sodium alginate compound built in). Sea plants with sodium alginate bind toxins in the intestinal tract, drawing from the body's cells. Adding seaweed to soups or bean dishes or as a snack is healthy for your thyroid. Coriander is also known as *cilantro* or *Chinese parsley*. It is a powerful antioxidant that has been demonstrated to remove heavy metals from the body. Incorporate cilantro in your recipes, such as the one below.

Some great ways to reduce exposure to heavy metals:
- Avoid the use of mercury in dental fillings.
- Use air filters and water purifiers in your home.
- Do not take antacids that contain aluminum hydroxide.
- Avoid using aluminum cookware.
- Do not use aluminum foil.
- Do not use antiperspirant spray, especially if it contains aluminum chlorohydrate.

Detoxification from heavy metals. Alginates from the brown seaweeds bind toxic metals to the digestive tract. Capsules combining sodium alginate from brown seaweeds and modified citrus pectin can be used every 3 months to reduce heavy metals. Cabbage, broccoli, Brussels sprouts, onions, and garlic all enhance detoxification and are ingredients in some of the recipes below.

Heavy Metal Detox Sauce

This is a healthy and delicious sauce that can be used on gluten-free pasta or rice, or as a dipping sauce for vegetables. The added benefit is that is removes heavy metals from the body. Double the recipe and freeze it in small containers so it can be pulled out for a quick healthy meal.

Ingredients

2 c. firmly packed organic cilantro leaves and stems

2 c. firmly packed organic Italian, flat leaf parsley leaves and stems

½ c. chopped organic walnuts

½ c. organic olive oil

1 tsp. kelp powder

¼ tsp. sea salt

2 garlic cloves

Directions

Using a food processor or blender, mix all ingredients together until smooth.

Coleslaw With Yogurt

Ingredients

2 c. shredded cabbage

½ c. chopped cauliflower

¾ c. shredded carrots

¼ c. toasted pecans

⅓ c. currants or raisins

10 drops stevia

2 tsp. fresh lemon juice

2 drops vanilla extract

½ c. plain full-fat yogurt

Directions

1. Combine the cabbage, cauliflower, carrots, pecans, and currants in a large bowl.
2. In a smaller bowl, whisk together the remaining ingredients and pour over the cabbage mixture, stirring well to combine.

Raw Cultured Vegetables

The fermentation process goes through two phases: The first phase is when the salty brine kills off harmful bacteria; the second phase is when the good lactobacillus bacteria convert sugars into lactic acid, which gives it that distinctly tangy flavor, and also acts as a preservative.

Ingredients

4 c. of vegetables, using a mixture of 3 parts cabbage and 1 part kale or other

vegetable, chopped (use organic vegetables that have been washed
and dried)

Water, as needed

Starter culture

3–5 cabbage leaves, whole

Directions

1. Chop the vegetables by hand and mix in a bowl.

2. Take several cups of the mixture and blend with water to make a brine (should be a thick liquid). Add the starter cultures to the brine.

3. Use an air-tight container, either glass or steel, with a rubber or plastic seal and a lid that clamps down. Add the remaining chopped veggies and brine to this jar, packing them in snuggly, leaving 2 inches at the top. Take the additional cabbage leaves, roll them up, and lay them across the top of the jar to fill this 2-inch space.

4. Let the jar sit for a minimum of 3 days at room temperature. It's best to let them sit for a week or more. The culture should be kept at around 70 degrees F. Warmer temperatures will speed up the culturing, so the vegetables will be ready in about half the time, but if it's too warm it's possible for the vegetables to spoil. If it's colder than 70 degrees, it may be necessary to insulate the container to keep it from getting too cold.

5. When the vegetables are done (you can taste them throughout the fermentation period to get a sense of this), place them in the refrigerator. They will stay good for up to 8 months.

Environmental Toxins in the Home and Kitchen

Environmental toxins are linked to a variety of mental health problems. Exposure to environmental toxins is especially dangerous for pregnant women and during the first years of life, but exposure at any stage is harmful. Although we cannot eliminate all exposures, we can reduce risk where we have control. This starts in the home with cleaning products and outside the home with pesticides or fertilizers, as well as detoxifying fruits and vegetables prior to consumption.

To eliminate pesticides and fertilizers from produce, fill a sink with water and add ½ cup of either hydrogen peroxide or one tablespoon of bleach. Let the vegetables and fruits soak for 5 minutes, then wash, rinse, and dry thoroughly.

Look underneath your sink and in your garage for toxic cleaning supplies, as well as drain and oven cleaners. If you have bought cleaning supplies in the store, they will be toxic, so throw them out. Replace them with a mixture of white or apple cider vinegar and water. Vinegar is a powerful antibacterial, antimold, and antifungal cleanser, and it is less expensive than commercial cleaners. If you like, add a little essential oil with your favorite fragrance. This mixture can be used to clean dishes, counters, floors, toilets, and tubs. If you need to scrub, just add some baking soda and salt. Also avoid dry cleaning.

STEP 4: MAKE A PLAN FOR SHORT- AND LONG-TERM CHANGE

Make a checklist.
- Prepare fresh food, and avoid packaged foods with preservatives and additives.
- Identify possible allergies and sensitivities and how they are affecting your well-being.
- Conduct elimination diets and other tests to assess for sensitivities.
- Identify the ratio of proteins, carbohydrates, and fats that makes you feel best, based on how fast you metabolize food: fast (carnivore), moderate (mixed foods), or slow (vegetarian based).
- Minimize exposure to toxic heavy metals.
- Undertake periodic cleanses to detoxify from heavy metals and toxins.
- Explore changes in your belief system regarding your dietary habits.

PART 3

Choose Good Mood Foods

CHAPTER 9

Plan Your Mood-Savvy Menu: The Best Foods for Mental Health

Foods either enhance mental health or make it worse. The key to mental health nutrition is to maximize the healthy, mood-savvy foods and minimize those foods that have a negative effect. Our goal for mental health nutrition is to have at least 90% of our recipes serve as nourishment for our brain, mind, and body. Identifying the best foods for you is your next step on the road to attaining mental well-being. Healthy foods and their preparation represent an essential part of a complete program for prevention of illness and recovery of mental health. Below I explore the value of mood-savvy foods and how to prepare them in numerous special recipes.

The Basic Pantry: 13 Essential Foods for Mental Health

- Bone broths
- Raw almonds
- Wild salmon or fatty fish
- Raw butter
- Coconut (meat and oil)
- Sweet potatoes
- Avocado
- Beets
- Cacao (chocolate)
- Oats and gluten-free grains
- Arugula and other bitter greens

- Fresh sauerkraut and other fermented foods
- Coffee/tea (green and black)

The above foods support mental health by:

- Maintaining healthy blood sugar
- Decreasing inflammation
- Boosting energy and mood
- Enhancing gut health, which supports mental health bacteria and neurotransmitters

---

DID YOU KNOW?

The absorption of nutrients in orange–red vegetables is significantly enhanced when combined with foods like avocado and avocado oil, which has been shown to enhance cognitive health. Thus the culinary practice of dipping raw carrot sticks in guacamole is an ideal combination for decreasing inflammation.

Mood-savvy foods also include healing sensory experience. For example, the smell of peppermint and using peppermint tea decreases headaches, and the citrus fruits like lemon and orange are antidepressant and reduce anxiety, as does cinnamon. The pleasant smells and tastes of mood-savvy foods improve our mood as well. The smell of a fresh orange reduces anxiety. Oranges (and other citrus) provide vitamin C, and the white pulp provides bioflavonoids that are powerful antioxidants.

SHOPPING LIST: THREE SUBSTITUTIONS TO MAKE FIRST

- Substitute brain health fats like butter, extra-virgin olive oil, and coconut oil for poor-quality fats.
- Substitute healthy sweets like stevia and raw honey for refined sugar and artificial sweeteners like aspartame.
- Substitute whole grains and root vegetables for refined carbohydrates like white flour.

COOKED FOOD OR RAW?

Some foods are best eaten cooked, while others are richest in nutrients when eaten raw or lightly cooked. Raw foods are an ideal way to increase your nutrient intake. Because heating food can decrease the amounts of nutrients and enzymes present in the food, raw foods will often provide more nutritional value to your diet and aid digestion. As a general rule, about 30%–50% of the diet should be eaten raw or slightly cooked. However, raw food is more difficult to digest, so if you are adding more raw foods to your diet, begin by adding in small amounts of lightly steamed or raw vegetables and fruits so you can adjust over a period of months. There are a number of ways to enjoy raw foods that range from a simple salad to an apple, or sprouting your own nuts and seeds.

MOOD-SAVVY FOOD PREPARATION

Cooking and food preparation should be fun, so choose your recipes based on your own enjoyment. The key to cooking for health is to stay in touch with what you enjoy eating and preparing. As you explore your mood-savvy diet and incorporating healthy foods and new preparation methods, remember that most of these recipes are easy and flexible. There is little that can go wrong with these recipes. There is no one right way to cook, so feel free to experiment and have a good time.

- Explore the foods of the "brainbow."
- Limit the amount of grains and legumes, and possibly eliminate glutens.
- Eat only high-quality, virgin, cold-pressed oils and fats.
- Eliminate refined carbohydrates like flour and sugars.
- Use proteins and root vegetables to stabilize mood and blood sugar.
- Include fermented foods in meals every day.
- Identify new foods from other cultures to eat for pleasure and mental health benefits.
- Emphasize organic, farm-raised, hormone-free, and antibiotic-free animal products.
- Share recipes and food prep with family and friends.

GOOD MOOD FATS

One of the first and easiest dietary changes to make to improve mental health is to change the types of fats you are using to beneficial fats. You will not be unhappy eating more butter and bacon. Fats are medicine for the brain, so when eating fats consider a selection of raw oils and saturated fats.

Seeds and Nuts

Raw seeds and nuts are excellent sources of fats and protein. Eat them raw, not roasted, although occasionally you can toast them lightly. They can also be soaked to make them more digestible. Nut and seed butters are an excellent snack for children at school, and for adults at work, especially when combined with apples or bananas. Sprinkle seeds or nuts on salads, add them to smoothies, or take them in the car or to school or office for a quick snack.

DID YOU KNOW?

Walnuts

According to ancient wisdom, the "doctrine of signatures" suggests that foods that look like parts of the body are medicine for that organ. Take a look at the walnut, which looks just like the brain! Modern research has shown that a handful of walnuts a day will improve memory.

Health-Savvy Raw Nuts and Seeds
- Sunflower seeds
- Pumpkin seeds
- Sesame seeds
- Chia seeds
- Walnuts
- Pecans
- Pistachios
- Hazelnuts
- Cashews

- Pine nuts
- Nut and seed butters

Nuts to Avoid
- Roasted nuts
- Peanut butter

HEALTHY SNACK

Cover almonds, walnuts, and organic dried fruit with water and place them in the refrigerator to soak overnight to make a nutritious sweet syrup. Use it to cover pancakes or cereal instead of other sweeteners. After using the syrup, put the nuts and fruit in a small container and carry it to school or work for a midday "pick-me-up."

CHIA AND NUT BUTTER SMOOTHIE

Ingredients

1 large ripe banana, peeled and frozen

1 c. unsweetened almond milk

1–2 tbsp. chia seeds

1 tbsp. raw almond butter (can substitute cashew or hazelnut butter)

1 tsp. coconut oil (optional)

¼ tsp. ground cinnamon (optional)

Directions

Put all of the ingredients in a blender and blend until smooth.

COCONUT MILK MOCHA

This is my favorite morning or afternoon guilt-free "pick-me-up." It is anti-inflammatory, rich in antioxidants, and provides brain food in the form of the trinity of cognitive function: coffee, cocoa, and coconut. If you prefer, you can substitute organic decaffeinated coffee or just use cocoa when serving to children, replacing the liquid from the coffee with extra coconut milk. Make sure your ingredients are organic and sugar-free.

Ingredients

12 oz. fresh brewed organic coffee, hot

½ c. full-fat, unsweetened coconut milk

2 tbsp. unsweetened organic cocoa powder (for drinking)

2–5 drops liquid stevia (or to taste)

Vanilla extract (optional)

Coconut cream, unsweetened (optional)

Directions

Combine all ingredients in a blender at medium speed for a few minutes until frothy. Pour into a mug and top with coconut cream, if desired.

Coconut

The coconut (*Coco nucifera*) is a nearly perfect food, rich in fats, protein, and a full complement of B vitamins. Coconut fat is used to produce energy, increase satiety, and may help with weight control and a reduction in body fat. Coconut fat does not slow digestion, as most fats do, nor does it circulate in the bloodstream to the degree that other fats do. Coconut oil is heat stable and thus is an excellent cooking oil and works especially well when cooking a vegetable stir fry. Buy organic, cold-pressed, unrefined coconut oil.

Try the following recipe, which uses coconut oil:

Vegetable Stir-Fry With Coconut Oil

This recipe is quite versatile since you can use any vegetables from the "brainbow" you choose. You can also add fish, shrimp, tofu, or beef to the dish.

Ingredients

4 tbsp. coconut oil

1 tbsp. toasted sesame oil (optional)

2 garlic cloves

2-inch piece raw ginger

2-inch piece raw turmeric

1 c. chopped onion

1 c. of broccoli

1 c. of raw cabbage

2 c. thinly sliced carrots

1 c. shiitake (or other mushrooms)

1 c. snow peas

Tamari, to taste

Directions

1. Gently heat the oil in a large frying pan.
2. The veggies in this recipe all take about the same time to cook, so once they are cut start adding them one at a time while you stir.
3. Near the end, add the mushroom. Cook until vegetables are soft.
4. If you are going to add fish, beef, or tofu, cook it in oil before the vegetables and then remove from the pan and set aside, adding to the cooked vegetables when they are done.

Optional: Freeze some tofu ahead of time. Then defrost and squeeze out excess water, cut into cubes, and add to the stir-fry. Frozen tofu becomes like a sponge and absorbs the juices and spices.

GOOD MOOD PROTEINS

Good mood proteins include various kinds of animal protein, bone broth, organ meats, fish, and cheese.

The following kinds of animal protein are beneficial:

- Grass-fed beef
- Organic chicken, turkey, and pork
- Antibiotic and hormone-free meats
- Humanely-raised animal meats
- Organ meats
- Bone broth
- Fresh wild salmon and other wild-caught fish
- Pickled herring, canned wild salmon, and sardines

These types of meats should be avoided:

- Grain-fed animal meats
- Farm-raised fish

Mood-Savvy Bone Broth

One of the first essential steps to include good quality protein in your diet is to make bone broth. Organic marrow and bones are inexpensive and yet are a very nutritious mood-savvy food. Bone broth is a traditional recipe that is both medicinal and nourishing. Its high mineral content makes it easy to digest and it is highly nutritious, especially the gelatin obtained from the bones. The broth also supports detoxification of the liver.

Ingredients

Raw marrow bones

Celery, carrots, onions, garlic, and parsley (but any vegetables will do)

Peelings and scraps, ends, tops, skins, or entire vegetable (If added toward the
  end of cooking, the mineral content will be higher)

Water

Apple cider vinegar or balsamic vinegar (2 tbsp. per quart of water, or per 2 lbs.
  of marrow bones)

Directions

1. Place bones in a Crock-Pot (or stove pot) over low heat and cover with water.
2. Heat the broth slowly and once the boil begins, reduce heat to its lowest point, so the broth just barely simmers. Scum will rise to the surface—skim this off.
3. Add vegetables or meat to broth during the last hour—or so that the vegetables are cooked but not mushy.
4. Broth should then be strained. The stock will keep several days in the refrigerator, or it may be frozen in plastic containers. Boiled down, it concentrates and becomes a jelly.

Organ Meats

Organ meats are an important source of nutrients and are an essential part of the savvy mood diet. Their source must be from grass-fed stock. Many epicurean foods today are made from the glands and organs of animals. There are quite a number of organ meat recipes available, such as the following:

• Liver pâtés / chopped liver
• Sautéed sweetbreads

- Menudo (soup made from tripe or stomach)
- Haggis (sheep stomach stuffed with cooked oats, blood, and organ meat)
- Blood pudding
- Kidneys
- Goat and pork testicles (affectionately called "oysters" or "huevos")
- Tongue (boiled and pickled)
- Heart
- Pancreas
- Headcheese (meat from a pig's or calf's head pressed into a gel)

When using animal proteins, use only humanely raised organic farm animals. This recipe draws on a tradition found the world over, where the liver of chicken (or cattle) is used to support health and well-being.

Chopped Liver

This is truly medicine for the liver and it is worth cultivating a taste for chopped liver, also known as Liver pâté. All of the ingredients—liver, eggs, onions, and duck (or chicken) fat—aid liver function. I then stuff the pâté into celery sticks, or romaine lettuce, top it with plenty of fresh parsley to enhance the flavor and to aid digestion of the fats, chill and it makes a meal.

Ingredients

2 large eggs - boiled

2 tbsp. unsalted butter

¼–½ cup rendered duck or chicken fat

1 onion, finely chopped

2 lbs. chicken livers

½ tsp Sea salt

¼ tsp freshly ground pepper

Celery sticks – 4 inch boats

Romaine Lettuce (optional)

Chopped parsley for garnish

⅛ tsp smoked paprika or cayenne pepper (optional)

Rendering chicken or duck fat

On the rare occasion that you might make roasted duck, this is a good time to render duck fat that will last you much of the year in the freezer. You can make this recipe with rendered chicken fat also, purchased in the store, but why not benefit from two birds in one net?

Rendering fat from a wild duck or farm raised chicken is important because fat is what stores the heavy metal toxins in our bodies. Mass produced fowl tend to contain more of such toxins. Similarly, as the major detoxifying organ of the body, chicken livers must be organic in order to be of benefit and not harmful.

Render Fat

1. Render fat by skinning the fowl and pulling fat from inside the cavity as well as the hind quarters. Chop the skins and fat into quarter inch pieces and place in a wide pan with water to cover. Start the process by heating the pan on high for about five minutes and then reduce to medium until the skin bits begin to sweat fat. Watch fairly carefully so as not to burn it, and continue to render until the bits begin to become soft cracklings. Pour off the fat into a small container and then add water to the pan again and continue to render once more until the water is evaporated. Pour off the remaining fat . . . and you have high quality rendered duck or chicken fat. Whatever you do not use for this recipe may be stored in small containers in the freezer.

Prepare the Livers

1. Place the eggs in cold water bring to a boil, and cook for 10 minutes. Let the eggs cool and place in the fridge for 30 minutes or until cold. Peel and chop.
2. In a large skillet, gently melt the butter in ¼ cup of the duck/chicken fat at a low heat. Add the onion and stir for about 10–15 minutes until caramelized. Place the livers on a sheet pan and roast in a 300 degree oven for about 12–15 minutes. At about 8 minutes check one of the livers by pressing on it. If they are soft but a little firm, they are ready. You want them to be pink inside, not overcooked and solid.
3. Place the liver and onions into the bowl of a food processor and let cool while you peel and chop the eggs. Pulse until the livers are finely chopped but not completely smooth. Test the flavor and texture to see if you want to add a little more fat and pulse again. Season to taste with sea salt and pepper.
4. Place the liver mixture in a bowl in the fridge and cover, or stuff the celery and wait 1–2 hours while your chopped liver rests and gets very cold. This can

also be made a day in advance. Sprinkle parsley leaves over the liver upon serving. For variations, sprinkle some smoked paprika or cayenne pepper for some *picante*.

Fish

Fish is an excellent source of protein. Only fish from wild sources should be used since farmed fish is often fed grains and can be toxic to health and the environment. The best fishes are fatty fish like fresh wild salmon. Other inexpensive sources of mood savvy fish are pickled herring, canned wild salmon, and sardines. Ask your local fishmonger to save you the fresh fish head and bones to make an excellent inexpensive broth.

Mood-Savvy Salmon Chowder

There is no better brain food than salmon. Among the Native peoples of the Pacific Northwest, the salmon is a spiritual being who brings nourishment and sustenance each year. Is it any wonder that there was little mental illness among people who ate a lot of salmon for their traditional diets? If you are able to get a whole salmon, begin by making a broth from the head, spine, fins, and gills. This preserves the benefits of the minerals from the bones and organs. For a chowder you can use the less expensive salmon, or even wild canned salmon from Alaska. But avoid using Atlantic or farmed salmon.

Ingredients

1 lb. fresh salmon, rinsed, patted dry, and cut into 1-inch pieces

2 tbsp. olive oil

1 medium onion, diced

2 cloves garlic, crushed or minced

2 medium stalks celery, sliced thin

¾ lb. baby potatoes, cut into ¼-inch pieces

2 c. salmon or chicken broth

1½ c. organic whole cream

2 tsp. sea salt, or to taste

¼ tsp. dried dill

Directions

1. Heat a large saucepan over medium heat. Add the olive oil, and then add onions and garlic. Sauté for about 2 minutes or until soft. Stir in celery and potatoes. Cook for about 3 minutes.

2. Add salmon or chicken broth. Heat to a simmer and then gently simmer until potatoes are almost tender, about 10–15 minutes.

3. Add the salmon (and corn kernels, if using) to the saucepan. Gently simmer for about 5 minutes or until the salmon is cooked through and the chowder has thickened slightly.

4. Add cream (optional) and sea salt to the saucepan.

5. Garnish with chopped parsley, and season with pepper and additional salt to taste.

Variations on this chowder include adding 2 cups of fresh (or canned) organic corn.

Cheese

The most nutritious cheese is derived from grass-fed, pasture-raised animals. Raw, unpasteurized cheese contains enzymes and healthy bacteria that improve digestion and also enhance the flavor of the cheese. Organic raw cheese from grass-fed animals is the best choice because it is free of antibiotics and growth hormones and is also higher in nutrients.

GOOD MOOD DAIRY

The following kinds of dairy products are beneficial:

- Full fat milk from pasture-raised cows
- Goat and sheep milk
- Goat cream and goat cheese
- Grass-fed, pasture-raised animal cheeses
- Aged cheeses
- Raw, unpasteurized cow or goat/sheep cheese

These types of dairy products should be avoided:

- Pasteurized milk and dairy products
- Homogenized and chemical-laden cow milk

There are many reasons not to use cow-based dairy milk products. Many people are allergic to cow milk, and it is associated with chronic ear infections and colds in children. Goat and sheep milk, goat cream, and goat cheese should be emphasized instead of cow milk and cheese.

Because so many people are allergic to casein, it is important to be aware of the following foods and ingredients that contain casein:

- Butter, butter flavoring, butter fat
- Calcium casein, casein hydrolysate, magnesium casein, potassium casein, rennet casein, sodium casein
- Cheese flavoring
- Custard
- Dairy products like cheese, yogurt, milk, kefir, ice cream, sour cream, half & half, and cream
- Lactalbumin, lactoalbumin phosphate, lactoglobulin, lactose
- Margarine
- Milk chocolate
- Nondairy creamers
- Powdered milk
- Protein powder
- Pudding
- Sherbert
- Whey, whey hydrolysate

You can then choose to use the following casein-free dairy and nondairy foods:

- Coconut butter
- Coconut milk
- Foods certified as kosher nondairy or pareve/parve ghee (look for *casein-free guaranteed*)
- Fruits and vegetables
- Italian ices
- Kosher pareve/parve foods
- Pareve/parve creams and creamers
- Proteins like meat and fish (read labels if processed or packaged)
- Rice, soy, nut, oat, or potato-based milks
- Sorbet (read label)
- Soy, rice, and coconut ice cream (not all flavors)
- Whole grains in their natural state

The following table shows the most common dairy foods and the alternative foods you can substitute for them:

Dairy Foods and Their Alternatives	
Dairy Foods	Substitutes
Cheese	Nondairy cheeses (made from nuts, hemp, soy,* and rice—look out for "casein" or "caseinate," a milk protein used in cheese substitutes, if you have a milk allergy as opposed to a lactose intolerance) Goat or sheep cheese (if tolerated) Nutritional yeast
Milk	Nondairy milks such as oat, coconut, cashew, hazelnut, almond, rice, and hemp milk Goat milk (if tolerated)
Kefir	Nondairy kefir products
Butter and margarine	Ghee (usually casein/lactose free), goat butter (if tolerated), coconut oil
Nondairy coffee creamer (contains casein)	Try coconut coffee creamers
Ice cream	Rice, hemp, coconut, or almond ice cream
Sour cream	Nondairy sour cream
Yogurt	Coconut, or rice yogurt with live cultures

* Unfermented soy contains antinutrients, such as saponins, soyatoxin, phytates, trypsin inhibitors, goitrogens, and phytoestrogens. It suppresses digestive enzymes and thyroid function. Soy should be avoided (except in the form of fermented soy products such as miso, shoyu, and tempeh—and then only in very small quantities and on rare occasions).

GOOD MOOD GREENS

Plant foods of all kinds, raw and cooked, should be used in the diet daily. Green plants are rich in chlorophyll, the green pigment in plants. Chlorophyll is called the "blood of plants" because its molecular structure is similar to hemoglobin, which is the molecule in red blood cells that transports oxygen through the blood. Chlorophyll inhibits bacterial and fungal growth, is anti-inflammatory, and helps to renew cells and support healthy gut function. Chlorophyll also helps to regulate calcium absorption. Chlorophyll is the "deodorizer" food. It is an energizing food important to people with fatigue-related conditions like chronic fatigue syndrome, adrenal fatigue, depression, fibromyalgia, and inflammatory bowel syndrome. Indeed, everyone needs chlorophyll. Chlorophyll is an excellent addition to a chocolate smoothie, but in moderation. While spinach, chard, and beet greens are high in chlorophyll, they are also high in oxalic acid that inhibits calcium absorption, so do not add too much.

See the following recipes for delicious, mood-elevating recipes that are also easy to prepare.

Salad Jar Meditation and Brain Bolt Dressing

People often complain to me about the time it takes to prepare fresh salads every day. I try to help them reframe their thoughts about time-consuming food preparation to considering salad-making as meditation. However, I also point out that it saves time to prepare salads for several days in advance. An easy way to prepare salads to have on hand for the week is to make salad jars. Family members, especially kids, enjoy placing vegetables in the jars. A pint-sized or quart-sized Mason jar can be used, depending on the size salad you want to make. Fill the jar with all the salad ingredients that you like. Layer the ingredients so that the dressing is at the bottom of the jar, the next level with heartier items that can withstand a little soaking, then vegetables, and finally the greens on top. Having the greens separate from the dressing keeps them from getting soggy. Anything that will be improved by soaking in the dressing, like a marinade, can go on the bottom—things like chicken, fish, tempeh, beans, quinoa, and mushrooms. Be sure to pack the jar tightly so that the ingredients don't shift around too much.

When you're ready to eat the salad, simply shake the jar a little bit, give it a stir, and enjoy!

Salad Jar Meditation

1. Shop for vegetables from all the colors of the "brainbow" that you will enjoy eating raw.
2. When you're ready to prepare your salad, put some meditation music on to get you in the moment-to-moment mood.
3. Wash all the vegetables and place them on the counter to dry as you prepare to cut them to bite size. Leave the skins on the vegetables unless they are waxed or bitter. Place each type of vegetable in bowls in a "buffet line" with the heavier, rooted vegetables like onions, carrots, and celery to the left,

and work your way up the line so the tomatoes and then the greens like kale, parsley, and lettuce are at the end when finished.

4. Make your salad dressing.
5. Place your jars in a line to the back of the vegetable bowls.
6. Add a layer of salad dressing to the bottom of each jar. Sprinkle different herbs such as dill, parsley, cayenne, or basil on top of the dressing.
7. Begin adding the heavier items on the left to the bottom of the jar and follow along, adding as you go, until you reach the end.

Note: Items like nuts and seeds may be placed at the bottom to soak in the dressing, or added separately when you open the jar.

Brain Bolt Dressing

One of the essentials of mental health is to make your own salad dressing. It can be simple or elaborate, but homemade can be medicine for the brain whereas store-bought dressings will never be. Nearly any dressing will do, but this is one of my favorites. You can make a jar of it and then add some different herbs each day so it is varied for your week of salads. This recipe makes about 2 cups of dressing.

Ingredients

¾ c. extra-virgin olive oil
¼ c. organic hemp oil
10 tbsp. balsamic vinegar
8 tbsp. raw apple cider vinegar
2 tbsp. dark agave, pure maple syrup, or raw honey
1 tsp. sea salt
2–3 minced cloves garlic, finely chopped
Freshly ground black pepper, to taste

Directions

Whisk all the ingredients together and store in a glass jar. Will keep for 1 week.
Optional add-ins: 4 tsp. Dijon mustard, 2 tsp. curry powder.

Mood-Savvy Salad

Every ingredient in this salad is rich and nourishing for the first and the second brain. The kale nourishes the microbiome, celery is a natural sedative, the beets and lemon support the gallbladder and mood, sea salt supports adrenal function, and the fats from avocado, olive oil, and walnuts nourish the mood and cognition. Eat this salad for lunch or dinner or use it as a raw side dish to a hearty stew.

Ingredients

1 bunch lacinato kale

1 tsp. sea salt

1 stalk celery, finely chopped

2 tsp. lemon juice

1 avocado, peeled and pitted

2 tbsp. olive oil

1–2 tsp. fresh minced garlic

½ c. shredded beets

Raw walnuts, as desired

Wedge of goat cheese (optional)

Directions

1. Remove stems and chop the kale leaves. Place them in a bowl and add the salt; gently rub the salt into the kale. Add celery and lemon juice and mix.
2. Mix the avocado and olive oil in a bowl with the minced garlic and pour over the salad, mixing well. Top the salad with beets and walnuts. Serve with goat cheese, if using.

Baked Kale Chips

Kale chips are a nutritious and incredibly tasty alternative to potato chips and other snacks. Try this basic recipe and then experiment with different spices. It makes 4–6 servings.

Ingredients

1 bunch kale

2 cloves garlic, minced

2 tbsp. extra-virgin coconut oil, melted

Sea salt, to taste

Cayenne pepper (optional)

Directions

1. Preheat oven to 350 degrees F.
2. Wash the kale and pat it dry. Remove the thick stems, coarsely tear the leaves, and put the leaves in a bowl.

3. Add garlic, oil, and sea salt (and cayenne pepper, if using); toss to coat. Alternatively, you can massage the oil and seasonings into the kale by hand.
4. Spread kale evenly on a baking sheet. Bake for 10–12 minutes, or until kale is crisp at the edges, being careful not to burn it.

Carrot Top Pesto

Pesto is a versatile sauce that brings vegetables, fish, or rice noodles to life. It is also medicine for the brain. Traditionally made with fresh basil and pine nuts, this recipe provides a way to use those beautiful carrot greens and at a fraction of the cost. Whereas pine nuts are expensive, walnuts are less so and they are a better brain food. Make a big batch of this pesto and freeze it in small containers to be available when you need a quick meal.

Ingredients

2 c. carrot tops, washed with stems removed
2 c. raw organic walnuts
2 cloves garlic
½ tsp. sea salt
⅔ c. olive oil
½ c. grated aged Parmesan cheese (optional if dairy-allergic)

Directions

1. Add carrot tops, walnuts, garlic, and salt to a food processor or high-speed blender.
2. Slowly pour in olive oil as you blend.
3. When you achieve a smooth consistency, add the Parmesan cheese and continue to process until smooth.

Healthy and Unhealthy Plant Foods

These are healthy plant foods:

- Sprouted seeds, beans, and grains
- Fermented soy products like tamari, shoyu, miso, and tempeh
- Cruciferous vegetables
- Root vegetables
- Leaves and stems
- Fruits
- Seaweed

These are plant foods to avoid:
- Unsprouted grains and beans
- Soybeans and isolated soy protein

MAKING SPROUTS AS A SAVVY FAMILY ACTIVITY

Sprouts are nutritious, inexpensive, and easy to incorporate into the diet. They provide enzymes and are high in vitamins, minerals, protein, fiber, and antioxidants. The process of making sprouts is easy, and fun, and children enjoy it.

Try these seeds, beans, and grains for sprouting:
- Seeds: Alfalfa, clover, broccoli, radish, fenugreek, sunflower, pumpkin, mustard, and onion seeds
- Beans: Mung beans, lentils, and chickpeas
- Grains: Millet, wheat, barley, brown rice, quinoa, buckwheat, rye, corn, oats, and wild rice

Sprouted alfalfa seeds are a good source of vitamins K and P, carotene, calcium, magnesium, potassium, sodium, iron, phosphorus, sulfur, silicon, cobalt, chlorine, zinc, and chlorophyll.

Broccoli and Other Cruciferous Vegetables

The vegetables of the cruciferous family are a wonderful source of fiber and can be eaten both cooked and raw. They contain glucoraphanin, which in concentrated amounts has been found to reverse oxidative stress and improve energy levels. The following delicious, mood–elevating recipes include cruciferous vegetables.

Pineapple-Cabbage Slaw With Chile-Coconut Dressing

Ingredients

Roasted Chile-Coconut Dressing/Sauce

½ c. organic extra-virgin coconut oil

4 generous tsp. coarsely ground chile or other flavorful medium-hot to hot ground chile

4 large garlic cloves, finely chopped

1⅓ c. full-fat coconut milk

2–2½ tsp. Asian fish sauce

¼ tsp. liquid stevia

¼–⅓ tsp. pink or gray sea salt

Juice of 1 to 1½ large limes

Salad

3–4 c. mixed greens

8 leaves napa cabbage, thinly sliced

4 whole scallions, thinly sliced

1½ c. fresh pineapple, cut into bite-sized pieces

½ c. dry-roasted and salted broken cashews

1½ to 2 c. cooked and diced tempeh, chicken, or seafood

½ c. fresh mint, coriander, or basil leaves, torn

Sea salt and fresh ground black pepper

Directions

1. To make the dressing, heat the coconut oil in a large sauté pan over medium heat. Add the chile and garlic and heat slowly for about 2 minutes, stirring often until the garlic is fragrant and sizzling, but not browned.

2. Add the coconut milk and increase heat, bringing the mixture to a boil. Allow it to boil for 30 seconds while stirring. Add 2 tablespoons of the fish sauce, the stevia, and the salt. Boil for 30 seconds, or until it is thickened, bubbly, and a rich caramel color.

3. Immediately transfer the sauce to a bowl. The sauce can be refrigerated for several days.

4. To make the salad, mix all the greens and cabbage in a bowl, then divide between four plates. Divide the remaining ingredients between each plate, tossing them over the greens. Season with salt and pepper.

5. If the sauce was made in advance, simply reheat it on the stove until bubbly, and then drizzle it over each salad. Squeeze fresh lime juice over the salads and serve.

Coconut Turmeric Cauliflower

This is a tasty recipe that satisfies, and reduces pain. Remember that turmeric needs black pepper to be adequately absorbed. The herbs and spices in this recipe can all be adjusted according to your palate. Kaffir lime leaves are a specialty item. If you can't locate some, substitute lime zest.

Ingredients

1 head cauliflower, cut into 1- to 2-inch florets

1 stalk lemon grass, or ¼–½ tsp. of lemon grass powder

3 tbsp. coconut oil

1 small onion, chopped

1-in. piece of ginger, peeled and chopped

6 (kaffir) lime leaves, or zest of a lime

1 tbsp. turmeric powder

½ tbsp. fresh ground black pepper

1 pinch sea salt

Directions

1. Turn the oven on to broil.

2. If using lemon grass, concentrate on the root where most of the flavor resides. Chop into ½-inch pieces. If using powder, add now to the oil in step 3.

3. Add 2 tablespoons of the coconut oil to a medium-sized pot and put on medium heat. Add the onion and ginger. Cook until soft. Add lemon grass and kaffir lime leaf. (if using zest, add only at the end of the cooking process. Lower heat and simmer for at least 30 minutes.

4. Toss the cauliflower and the remaining coconut oil together in a bowl with sea salt. Place in a baking dish and put in the oven to broil until it is lightly browned.

5. Strain the lemon grass mixture, and drizzle the sauce over the cauliflower. Add sea salt and turmeric, tossing until the cauliflower is thoroughly coated and a lovely yellow color.

Stuffed Cabbage

My grandmother Esther would call this recipe a *patchke*—a lot of work. It does take some time, but it's worth it. Take your time, make a double recipe, and freeze the leftovers.

Ingredients

For the sauce:

3 tbsp. extra-virgin olive oil

1½ c. chopped onion (2 onions)

6 chopped tomatoes with juice

¼ c. red wine

1 tbsp. raw honey

½ c. raisins

1½ tsp. sea salt

¾ tsp. freshly ground black pepper

1 large head savoy or green cabbage, including outer leaves,
  core removed

½ c. pine nuts (optional)

For the filling:

2½ pounds ground beef or lamb

3 eggs, lightly beaten

½ c. finely chopped onion

½ c. brown rice (or other grain of choice)

1 tsp. minced fresh thyme leaves

1 tsp. sea salt

½ tsp. freshly ground black pepper

Directions

1. To make the sauce, heat the olive oil over medium-low heat and cook the onions until translucent, 5–10 minutes. Add the tomatoes with their juice, wine, honey, raisins, salt, and pepper. Turn the heat up and bring to a boil, then return to low heat and simmer 30 minutes, uncovered. Stir occasionally. Set aside.

2. While the sauce is cooking, bring a large pot of water to a boil.

3. Immerse the head of cabbage in the boiling water for a few minutes, peeling off each leaf with tongs as soon as it is soft. Set the leaves to the side.

4. For the filling: in a large bowl, combine the ground beef, eggs, onion, brown rice, thyme, salt, and pepper. Add 1 cup of the sauce to the meat mixture.

5. Preheat the oven to 350 degrees F.

6. To assemble, cut out the hard triangular rib from the base of each cabbage leaf with a small paring knife. Spread 1 cup of the sauce in the bottom of a large glass baking dish. Place ⅓ to ½ cup of filling in an oval shape near the rib edge of each leaf and roll up toward the outer edge, tucking the sides in as you roll. Place half the cabbage rolls, seam side down, over the sauce. Add more sauce and more cabbage rolls until all the cabbage rolls are in the pot, and cover with the remaining sauce. Cover the dish tightly with the lid and bake for 90 minutes or until the meat is cooked and the rice is tender. Sprinkle the pine nuts before serving hot.

Sea Vegetables (Seaweeds)

Seaweeds are a rich source of vitamins, minerals, proteins, lipids, and amino acids. They are one of the best foods by which to obtain minerals, including calcium, phosphorus, magnesium, iron, iodine, and sodium. They are especially rich in iodine, which is essential for healthy thyroid function and a good mood. The high mineral content of seaweeds supports nervous system function, good mental health, and muscle relaxation and function.

Savvy Seaweed Salad

This salad is an ideal introduction to seaweed. It is mild in taste, and just a few tablespoons provide a rich assortment of minerals and vitamins.

Ingredients

1 c. dry arame or hijiki seaweed

Scallions

Tofu

Carrot

Pea pods

Red pepper

English cucumber

Few pieces chopped broccoli florets

Chopped walnuts or pine nuts

Chopped sprouts (optional)

¼ c. toasted sesame oil

¼ c. rice wine vinegar

Small piece fresh ginger

1 garlic clove

1 tbsp. tamari/wheat-free soy sauce

Hot red pepper flakes (optional)

Directions

1. Soak the seaweed in warm water for 15 minutes until soft (save the water for soup or to put in your animal companion's bowl)

2. Dice the scallions, tofu, carrots, pea pods, red pepper, cucumber, broccoli, nuts, and sprouts into small (equal-size) pieces.

3. Combine this mixture with the softened seaweed.

4. Mix the toasted sesame oil, rice wine vinegar, and tamari together and pour over the seaweed-vegetable mixture. Squeeze the juice from 2 cloves of garlic and a good-sized chunk of fresh ginger and mix into the dressing. Mix and allow to marinate for a few hours. Sprinkle with hot red pepper flakes (optional). Eat and enjoy!

Plant Protein Smoothies

There are times when we need to make a quick meal that has all the nutrients necessary for a savvy mood—times like the following:

- No time to prepare a regular meal
- Need to take a meal to work or for travel
- Children are late for school and they need a meal for their thermos
- Need an alternative to taking pills, and we want to blend our nutrients
- Want a special liquid treat that includes blended chocolate and coffee

The following plant- and dairy-derived proteins are ideal to have on hand along with powdered vitamins, minerals, and liquid omega-3 fats:

- Hemp protein
- Hemp seeds
- Microalgae (spirulina, chlorella, wild blue-green algae)
- Pea protein
- Whey protein
- Frozen bananas, berries, or mangos
- Almond, hemp, or coconut milk
- Goat yogurt or kefir
- Liquid stevia
- Powdered organic cocoa
- Vitamins and oils
- Protein powders

Fruity Turmeric Smoothie

Ingredients

½ c. frozen pineapple or mango

1 fresh banana

1 c. milk (hemp or coconut milk)

1 tbsp. coconut oil, melted

½ tsp. turmeric, fresh

½ tsp. cinnamon

½ tsp. ginger, fresh

¼ tsp. ground black pepper

1 tsp. chia seeds

1 tsp. green tea powder (optional)

¼ c. goat yogurt (optional)

1 tsp. raw honey or 10 drops of liquid stevia (optional)

Directions

1. Add ingredients to a blender in the following order: frozen fruit, banana, milk, oil, spices, and remaining ingredients.

2. Blend until smooth.

Avocado–Coconut Smoothie (Makes 2 servings)

Ingredients

1 avocado

1 banana (fresh or frozen)

1 c. coconut milk (full fat)

½ c. orange juice

2 tbsp. freshly squeezed lime juice

1 pinch salt

1 tsp. honey or 1–2 drops liquid stevia extract (optional)

Directions

1. Peel the avocado and remove the pit. Cut it into chunks and place in a blender.

2. Peel the banana, break in two, and place in the blender.

3. Add the remaining ingredients (and honey or stevia, if using) to the blender, and blend until smooth, or about 1 minute.

4. Pour into two large glasses and serve.

Legumes

Legumes are the edible dry fruits and seeds contained in shells and pods. They include beans, lentils, peas, and peanuts. Beans are a good source of protein and are rich in potassium, iron, B vitamins, and calcium.

There are various processes you can use to make legumes more beneficial:

- Sprouting legumes increases their digestibility as well as their vitamin C and enzyme levels.
- Soaking beans before cooking reduces their cooking time and begins the sprouting process, which increases their nutritional benefit and reduces their gas–producing enzymes.
- Cooking beans with fats helps to increase their digestibility.
- Adding seaweed to beans increases their nutritional benefit, flavor, and digestibility, as well as reducing cooking times.

SOAKING LEGUMES AND NUTS

Legumes should be soaked before cooking (and soaked before sprouting), and nuts may be soaked to enhance digestibility.

Legumes

1. Place the legumes in a bowl and cover with warm water.
2. For each cup of beans, add 1 tablespoon apple cider vinegar (do not add vinegar to lentils or split peas).
3. Soak at room temperature for a minimum of 7 hours. Larger beans should be soaked for 24 hours, changing the water only if they begin to ferment.
4. After soaking, drain and cook according to directions.

Spice with black pepper, fennel, and cumin to reduce the gas-producing effects of beans. Salt should be added only at the end of cooking. Apple cider vinegar can also be added at the end of cooking to soften beans and increase their digestibility.

Nuts

1. To soak nuts, simply cover in warm water and soak for 7 hours.
2. Drain the nuts and let sit at room temperature to dry out, or store in the fridge and use as needed. Only soak as many nuts as you will eat in a 24-hour period.

Split Pea Soup with Sausage or Tofu

You can't go wrong with this soup. It is simple and quick to make in a Crock-Pot, and perfect for those who prefer sausages to vegetables. (Healthy organic hot dogs will do for the kids in the crowd.) It is a great way to enjoy a nourishing soup filled with mood-boosting minerals and proteins. You can add different vegetables as you wish. The soup is a meal in itself and can be complemented with sourdough bread or raw salad. The great thing about this soup is that you can keep it in the Crock-Pot all day on warm so that family members can fill a bowl whenever they want. It takes about 20 minutes to clean and prep all the ingredients.

Ingredients

6–8 c. of liquid (bone, chicken, or vegetable broth)

2 c. dried green peas, soaked and rinsed

1 c. thickly sliced carrots

1 c. thickly sliced celery

1 medium onion, sliced

2 c. chopped kale

2 cloves garlic, optional

2 marrow bones and 4 organic sausages sliced into 1-inch rounds (for a
  vegetarian soup, substitute frozen, thawed tofu*)

*Tofu has a wonderful consistency when it is frozen and thawed. It is like a sponge that absorbs flavors. Freeze tofu, let thaw, and gently press out the excess water— then cube and use as desired in soups and stir-fries.

Directions

1. Soak the split peas in warm water overnight before cooking in order to reduce the phytates, which inhibit absorption of minerals.
2. After soaking, rinse and add the liquid to the broth. Place the soaked peas in the Crock-Pot with 8 cups of broth (as a general rule, use 3 cups of water to each cup of dried lentils or peas). Cook on low heat for 3 hours or until peas are soft.
3. Add all the vegetables and sausage (or tofu) and cook for another 1–2 hours.
4. Add some salt and crushed rosemary or thyme when the soup is done and let sit until ready to eat.

Antidepressant Dhal

This nightshade-free soup is rich in anti-inflammatory and antidepressant spices and foods. It is nourishing and easily digested.

Ingredients

4 c. water

1 c. (red, brown, or green) lentils

1 tsp. cumin seeds

1 tsp. fenugreek powder

1 tsp. cardamom powder

3 tbsp. ghee or raw butter

1 onion, diced

1 carrot, sliced

1 sweet potato, diced

2-inch piece fresh turmeric, chopped

4 cloves garlic, minced

2-inch piece fresh ginger, chopped

Grey or pink sea salt, to taste

½ tsp. freshly grated black pepper

1 can of coconut milk

1 c. chopped cilantro (plus extra for topping)

2 c. of cooked brown rice

Chopped cilantro, goat yogurt, and chopped green onions
    to top each bowl for serving

Directions

1. Bring a pot of water to a boil. Add the lentils, reduce heat to a simmer, and cook for about 20 minutes until the water is reduced and the lentils are very soft. Add the cumin seeds, fenugreek, and cardamom, and keep warm.

2. Heat the ghee in a large saucepan. Add the onions, carrots, and sweet potatoes, and sauté until the onions are translucent and the sweet potatoes are soft. If they start to stick, add a little water. Add the turmeric, garlic, and ginger in the last 5 minutes of cooking.

3. Add the vegetables to the red lentils and spices, and mix together. Add the coconut milk and cilantro and gently heat.

4. Serve over brown rice and top with additional chopped cilantro, goat yogurt, and chopped green onions.

GOOD MOOD CARBOHYDRATES

Carbohydrates to include in the diet are:

- Grains, soaked and cooked
- Legumes (legumes are both carbohydrates and plant protein)
- Vegetables, raw and cooked—those that grow above ground and below ground
- Fruits, raw and dried (sulfite-free and organic)

Grains

We cannot digest grains efficiently; however, we can *predigest* them, which is why all traditional cultures either soak or ferment grains. For example, sourdough culture is used to prepare bread, and this neutralizes the phytic acid, making it more digestible and increasing its nutrient content.

Adding generous amounts of fat (like butter) to grains protects the gut from fiber damage and increases the absorption of important fat-soluble nutrients in the grains.

SOAKING AND COOKING GRAINS

Soaking grains before cooking them shortens the cooking time, releases nutrients, and increases their digestibility.

1. Wash grains.
2. Place grains in a bowl and cover with warm water.
3. For each cup of grain, add 1 tablespoon apple cider vinegar or lemon juice.
4. Soak at room temperature for 8 to 12 hours.
5. Drain the water from the grains, place them in a cooking pot, and fill with fresh water according to specific grain-to--water ratios. Add about ¼ tsp. of sea salt per cup of grain, or add seaweed.
6. Bring the water to a boil, reduce heat to low, cover, and cook according to specific grain cooking times. Cooking time may be reduced by as much as half after soaking, so check the grains halfway through.

Black Rice Breakfast Pudding With Coconut and Fruit (Serves 3–4)

Ingredients

1 c. black rice, soaked overnight

1 can coconut milk (full-fat)

¼ tsp. fine grain sea salt

½ vanilla bean, seeds and pod (optional)

½ c. water

1 tbsp. maple syrup, raw honey, or raw agave

⅓ c. coconut flakes, lightly toasted

Mango, raspberries, blueberries, pomegranate, banana, kiwi, pineapple, or other fruit of your preference

Directions

1. Cover the rice with water and soak overnight or for up to 8 hours. Drain and rinse.
2. Combine the rice in a pot with the coconut milk, salt, vanilla bean, and the ½ cup of water. Bring to a boil, reduce to a simmer, and cover. Cook, stirring frequently, until the rice is tender and most of the liquid has been absorbed (you still want a little liquid), about 25–30 minutes.
3. While the rice is cooking, prepare all the fruit that you would like to accompany the pudding.
4. When the rice is done cooking, remove from the heat and gently stir in the maple syrup, honey, or agave.
5. Serve the black rice in bowls, and top with the fruit and toasted coconut.

Congee

A traditional Chinese recipe, congee is a rice porridge cooked with lots of water for a long amount of time. It is a comfort food that promotes strong digestion and is easily assimilated, in addition to being easy and affordable to make. You can increase its medicinal properties by adding other beneficial vegetables, grains, legumes, and medicinal or culinary herbs. These ingredients will also be more easily digested and assimilated when cooked with the rice and water.

Ingredients

1 c. grain (usually white or brown rice)

5 to 6 c. liquid (broth or water)

Pinch of sea salt

Optional: a handful of raisins, 1 tsp. of cinnamon or finely chopped ginger, and broccoli

Directions

1. If you are using a Crock-Pot, add the ingredients and set to low, leaving it on overnight.
2. If you are using the stovetop, add the ingredients to a stockpot, cover, and bring to a boil. Reduce heat to very low and simmer for four to six hours.

Too much water is better than too little, and the longer the congee cooks, the better it gets.

Mushroom Risotto

I love all risotto recipes because they require that I engage my patience. It can become a meditation to gather and prepare everything that goes into the risotto, and then the stirring—the gentle, rhythmic, mindful stirring is in itself relaxing. Invite friends over to share because there will be enough for several plates. Then the treat is sitting down to eat the comforting richness of a smooth risotto that warms the heart and belly. Pair the risotto with a green salad of bitter greens to help digest the brain-healing fats.

Note: If alcohol is contraindicated, just leave it out.

Ingredients

5–6 c. chicken stock

2 tbsp. butter

2 c. of shiitake and oyster mushrooms, cleaned, trimmed, and cut into half-inch or 1-inch pieces

⅓ c. finely chopped sweet onion

1¾ c. arborio rice

⅔ c. brandy or dry white wine

⅓ c. freshly grated Parmesan cheese

Sea salt and freshly ground black pepper, to taste

2 tbsp. chopped fresh parsley

Directions

1. Bring stock to a simmer in a saucepan.
2. Melt the butter in a deep, heavy, medium-sized saucepan over medium-high heat. Add mushrooms and onions and sauté about 5 minutes. Add the rice and stir to combine.
3. Add brandy, bring to a boil, and reduce liquid by half, about 3–4 minutes. Add simmering stock, ½ cup at a time, stirring enough to keep the rice from sticking to the edges of the pan. Stir the rice almost constantly—stirring sloughs off the starch from the rice, making the creamy sauce you are looking for in a risotto. Wait until the stock is almost completely absorbed before adding the next ½ cup. This process will take about 25 minutes. The rice should be just cooked and slightly chewy.
4. Stir in the Parmesan cheese and season to taste with salt and pepper. Garnish with chopped fresh parsley or chives.

GOOD MOOD FRUITS

Most people will do well eating at least 1–2 pieces of raw fruit each day. Because fruits are an excellent source of fiber as well as easily absorbed sugars, vitamins, and minerals, they are an ideal food to regulate digestion and elimination. They also make a good transitional food if you are withdrawing from sugar addiction, because the fiber slows the absorption of fructose. The best principles for fruit selection are to choose different fruits according to the colors of the fruit "brainbow," and to eat fruits when in season.

Dried Fruits

As an alternative to fresh fruit, dry fruits are also a good source of fruit, especially during the winter months. When combined with raw nuts they make a perfect midmorning snack at work, or for children at school.

Dry fruits are high in fiber and minerals and provide excellent support for digestion and elimination. Choose from figs, prunes, raisins and apricots. The sugar is concentrated, so eat only small amounts. Because sulfites can cause respiratory distress and mood changes, it is essential to purchase only organic, sulfite-free and preservative-free dried fruits.

Consider purchasing a dehydrator and dry your own fruits. This is very cost effective, especially if you harvest fruits during the summer and dry them for year-round storage. Dried fruits keep well in the freezer.

Fruit Recipes

Figs, Carrots, and Pine Nuts Over Couscous

Figs are the center piece of this dish, which celebrates a blending of flavors reminiscent of the Mediterranean. The figs are a good source of potassium and healthy sweetness, filled with fiber; and the pine nuts are a good source of protein. Couscous is made from durum wheat that has been steamed and dried. It is mild and adaptable, forming a wonderful base for any well-seasoned juicy dish like this because it absorbs all the flavors. This recipe is a forgiving one; even though it looks complicated, you cannot go wrong.

Ingredients

3 tbsp. unsalted butter

2 medium carrots, grated

½ tsp. ground cinnamon

2 c. couscous

1 c. chopped organic figs (about 6 oz.)

1¼ c. water

1 c. fresh chicken (or vegetable) broth

1 tsp. sea salt

¼ tsp. ground black pepper

¾ c. raw or lightly toasted pine nuts

3 tbsp. minced fresh parsley

½ tsp. orange zest

1 tbsp. orange juice

Directions

1. Heat butter in medium saucepan over medium-high heat. Add the grated carrots and ½ teaspoon ground cinnamon; cook, stirring frequently, until carrots soften, about 2 minutes.

2. Add couscous and figs and cook, stirring frequently, until grains are just beginning to brown, about 5 minutes.

3. Add water, broth, and salt and pepper; stir briefly to combine, cover, and remove pan from heat. Let stand until grains are tender, about 7 minutes.

4. Uncover and fluff grains with fork.

5. Stir the toasted pine nuts, fresh parsley leaves, orange zest, and orange juice into couscous before serving.

Arugula–Fig–Peach Salad

The Buddha "saw the light" while sitting under a fig tree, perhaps because he was eating the tryptophan-rich figs that were dropping all around him. Besides boosting the happiness-linked amino acids like tryptophan, figs are rich in antioxidants and minerals, making them a super "brainbow" food. The combination of sweet fruit and bitter greens in this end-of-summer salad awaken the senses and stimulate joy. Add some nuts, thinly sliced hard cheese, or crisped serrano ham to make a whole meal to share with your mood-elevating friends.

Ingredients

6 ripe figs

3 ripe peaches

Arugula (half a bunch)

Fresh parsley sprigs

Sea salt

Directions

1. Wash and dry the greens, and then drizzle virgin olive oil very lightly over them.
2. Sprinkle salt over the greens, then toss and set them aside.
3. Cut the peaches into slices and halve the figs.
4. Heat some olive oil in a pan and when hot, place the figs cut-side-down in the plan and sear for 10 seconds only.
5. Remove the figs and cool; then top the greens with the fruit, lightly drizzle balsamic vinegar, toss, and serve.

Succulent Prunes in Cognac

What could be better for one's mood than a little caffeine and relaxed, efficient elimination at the same time? My friend and super chef Peggy Knickerbocker developed this recipe, and I have adapted it here for mental health. It combines prunes, Armagnac (a brandy similar to Cognac) and Lapsang souchong tea. Lapsang souchong is a smoky black tea with moderate caffeine content, and prunes are well known for their laxative effect. The touch of Armagnac (optional) adds an elegant and restful element. It is also a very exotic dessert for a party.

Ingredients

1 lb. pitted prunes

1 large piece of orange zest, 1 in. by 3 in.

2-in. section of fresh ginger, unpeeled

2 c. Lapsang souchong, Earl Grey, or other hot brewed tea

10 drops of stevia or 1 tbsp. of raw honey

Juice of 1 large orange

2 cinnamon sticks

½ c. Armagnac or Cognac

1 c. crème fraîche or Greek yogurt

Directions

1. Place the prunes, orange zest, and ginger in a nonreactive saucepan and pour the tea over them. Soak for at least 1 hour or overnight.
2. Pour off all but about ⅓ cup of the tea from the prunes.

3. Add the stevia (or honey), orange juice, cinnamon sticks, ½ cup water, and the cognac. Simmer over low heat for 10 to 15 minutes. Remove the ginger.

4. Spoon the prunes into small bowls and serve with a dab of crème fraîche or Greek yogurt on top.

SPECIAL MENTAL HEALTH FOODS

There are many special foods that improve mental well-being because they improve physical health. Among these are plants called *bitter greens*, which include dandelions, arugula, mustard leaves, and watercress.

The liver loves bitter plants and foods because they aid the digestion of fats. Eat some bitter plants with a high-fat meal to enhance fat digestion.

Chocolate/Cocoa

Chocolate is sometimes called "the food of the gods," and for good reason—when consumed without sugar it is anti-inflammatory and high in polyphenols. Cocoa increases circulation and blood vessel growth, improving blood flow to the brain and supporting cognitive function and memory. Cocoa improves mood and also stimulates healthy microbiota production in the gut.

Chocolate Lamb Chili

Lamb is often a special treat and one worth waiting for. People may find the taste of lamb a little strong, but that's often because it was an older lamb or did not have much fat on it. This chili is a great way to integrate a less expensive cut of lamb into your diet while enjoying our favorite mood foods—like chocolate, beans, and chili spices. This whole meal can be made in the Crock-Pot, but some preparation of the lamb will be necessary before placing the ingredients in the Crock-Pot. You can also leave out the lamb and make it vegetarian-style, or with beef. Pinto beans tend to be easier to digest than other beans, and the vinegar adds to the digestibility of this meal.

Ingredients

1 c. dry pinto beans
½ tbsp. ground coriander
2 tsp. ground cumin
1 tsp. dried oregano
½ tsp. dried thyme

½ tsp. ground cardamom

1 tbsp. prepared yellow mustard

1 lb. boneless leg of lamb cut into ½-in. pieces

3 tbsp. virgin olive oil

2 large yellow onions, diced

⅛ c. organic white vinegar

2 cloves garlic, minced

3 chipotles in adobo, diced

2 qt. lamb, beef, or chicken broth

2 tbsp. of organic cocoa powder

Sea salt to taste

Ground pepper to taste

5 sprigs of fresh cilantro, chopped

Directions

1. Pour 1quart of stock (lamb, beef, or chicken) over the pinto beans—the stock should cover about 2 inches above the beans—in a Crock-Pot.
2. Cook for 2–3 hours on high or until tender.
3. When completed, turn the Crock-Pot to warm, and reserve the beans in a bowl.
4. Place the lamb in the Crock-Pot covered with broth. If you do not have enough broth, add water—the lamb will create its own broth as it cooks.
5. Place the olive oil in a sauté pan, add the garlic and onions, and cook to light brown.
6. Then add chipotles in adobo, and as they cook gently stir in ground coriander, ground cumin, oregano, thyme, and ground cardamom.
7. Lightly brown lamb pieces in the sauté pan, then transfer to the Crock-Pot. Cover and cook for 2½ hours on medium.
8. Once the lamb is well cooked, stir in the beans, cover, and cook just until they have warmed through.
9. Stir in the yellow mustard, vinegar, and chocolate, mixing thoroughly.
10. Season with sea salt and ground pepper, and top with cilantro.
    (If you want more *wow* to the chili, top with a pinch of cayenne pepper once it is in the bowls.)

Add a bitter greens salad to make it a complete healthy-mood meal.

Berries

Berries are in the red-blue-purple spectrum of the "brainbow" and are among the most versatile antioxidants. In the summer they can be picked fresh, and during the winter months they can be stored in the freezer. Make them the fruit of choice in smoothies or as toppings to gluten-free pancakes. For a special treat, dip strawberries into stevia-sweetened melted dark chocolate.

GOOD MOOD FOODS AROUND THE WORLD

Every culture has special foods and recipes to enhance mental well-being. Below are a few of these foods and recipes that are easy to find in the United States. However, don't stop here. Make a list of the favorite foods of your family and friends, organize a savvy-mood cultural heritage party to celebrate the gifts that different cultures offer for our brain and mind, or try some of these special cultural mood foods:

- Plantains (India, Africa, Caribbean countries, Mexico)
- Prickly-pear cactus (Mexico)
- Yuca/cassava
- Roselle (Africa, Jamaica, Mexico)
- Watermelon (worldwide)

Plantains

Plantains are members of the banana family and often overlooked as a food source in the United States. They can be found in the specialty produce section of your supermarket and at Mexican and Asian food stores. They peel like a banana and should be ripe or moderately soft. They offer a natural earthy sweetness that can be seasoned as savory or sweet. They are easily digested, which makes them ideal for the elderly or people who are ill. Plantains make an excellent addition to the starchy carbohydrate reper-toire, especially when eliminating sugar or wheat from the diet. They can be sliced thin, fried in coconut oil, and served as chips; they can be steamed and added to a vegetable dish, or topped with butter; they can be grilled, and also used in a curry. My favorite way to eat plantains is in this soup recipe, which also combines coconut and the tang of cilantro (Chinese parsley) to enhance brain function.

Plantain Soup

Ingredients

3 large plantains, peeled and cut into ½ in. slices

Juice from ½ lemon

3 tbsp. unsalted butter

1 medium onion, chopped

5 cloves garlic, minced

4 c. freshly made chicken or vegetable broth

Sea salt and black pepper, to taste

1 c. coconut milk

Toppings

⅓ c. cilantro

1 clove garlic, chopped

1 tsp. grated orange peel

3 tbsp. lime juice

Directions

1. Place plantains in a bowl; sprinkle with lemon juice to preserve their color.
2. Heat butter in a saucepan on medium heat. Add the onion and the 5 cloves of garlic and sauté until onion is tender, about 5–10 minutes.
3. Add plantains and chicken broth and bring to a boil. Reduce heat to low, add salt and pepper, and simmer until plantains are tender, about 25–30 minutes.
4. Place mixture in a blender and puree just until smooth—do not overblend. Return to saucepan and add coconut milk. Cook over low heat for 5 minutes to heat through.
5. In a blender or food processor, blend cilantro, garlic, orange peel, and lime juice. After blending, swirl this mixture into the bowl of soup when serving.

Prickly-Pear Cactus

The paddles of the prickly pear cactus, also known as the *nopal cactus*, are called *nopales*. They are an inexpensive, delicious food for mental health known to reduce blood glucose levels and soothe digestion. They are found in the produce section or at Mexican food stores. Have fun with the following recipe, and you will also impress your friends and family with an exotic dish.

Nopales and Eggs

This recipe makes a nourishing dish for any time of day. Set aside half a cup of raw nopal and use it in your smoothie the next day.

Ingredients

4 paddles of nopal cactus

3 cloves garlic, minced

1 large onion, chopped

⅓ c. olive oil

¼ tsp. baking soda

5 large eggs

1 pinch pepper, to taste

1 pinch sea salt, to taste

Directions

1. Carefully remove the spines from each nopal paddle and then julienne it into ¹/₁₆-inch slices.
2. Place garlic, onions, and olive oil in a 10-inch fry pan. Cook over medium-high heat until onions are translucent.
3. Add the nopal to the onion-garlic mixture, then the baking soda, and stir the mixture frequently.
4. Whip eggs in a separate bowl.
5. When the nopal turns lighter green, stir in the whipped eggs. Add pepper and salt to taste. When eggs are set, serve.

Yuca

Yuca, also known as *tapioca* or *cassava*, can be used in place of potatoes when eliminating nightshade foods from the diet. It is similar in texture to the potato and makes a good substitute in recipes. The best way to buy yuca is from a Vietnamese or Asian market where they sell cleaned, frozen packs of cassava. Remove it from the package, boil it in water for 10–15 minutes, slice it in half, pull or cut out the tough and stringy core, and it is ready for use. Yuca has anti-inflammatory and antioxidant properties.

Roselle Jell-O

The roselle plant was brought to Jamaica by Africans during the slave trade and from there it became part of subtropical western diets. Found commonly in Mexican groceries and called Jamaica (with Spanish pronunciation), it is a powerful and inexpensive brain antioxidant. Who doesn't remember a dessert of Jell-O and love its cool, soothing texture? Gelatin is a superfood for joints, skin, and energy, but commercial Jell-O is packed with sugar and should be avoided. This recipe combines healthy gelatin with coconut and fruit, and it can be made with a variety of fruit variations.

Ingredients

1 c. of dried Jamaica petals

1½ c. of boiling water

1 tbsp. pasture-raised gelatin

¼ c. of hot water

1 c. of fresh diced fruit

10 drops of stevia

Directions

1. Boil 1 cup of water and pour over the Jamaica petals. Set aside until warm.
2. Strain the petals, pour the warm liquid into a large mixing cup, and add the gelatin powder.
3. Add the ¼ cup of really hot water and stir until it is thinner.
4. Stir briskly until mixed—it will start to thicken.
5. Place the fruit into an 8 × 8 glass baking dish. Pour the Jell-O mixture over the fruit and make sure it has coated the fruit.
6. Put in the fridge, covered, for at least 3 hours, or leave overnight, and serve with coconut milk, real whipped cream, or top with sliced almonds.

Watermelon

Use watermelon generously for depression. It is rich in vitamin B_6 which aids the happiness neurotransmitter serotonin. Sweet fruits are a good alternative to refined sugar, as a transitional food. Save the watermelon rinds, which are rich in chlorophyll, and make them into pickles. Below I provide two different watermelon drinks designed to lift your spirits.

Spring-In-Your- Step Refresher (Serves 2)

1. All the ingredients in this drink elevate the mood. The fresh ginger and mint leaves are stimulants and also help stress headaches. Use only large, organic watermelons with seeds, not the small, hybrid, seedless variety. The seeds will grind up and they add a Vitamin B and Magnesium fiber- rich crunch to this mood-boost beverage.

2. Plan ahead and make this beverage in advance, as the flavors blend and flavor is enhanced over several hours.

Ingredients

4 cups of watermelon

3 tbsp fresh squeezed lime juice

¼ tsp raw, peeled, chopped ginger

6 fresh mint leaves (or ¼ drop of edible peppermint oil)

Directions

1. In blender or food processor, puree the watermelon, lime juice, and ginger. Transfer to a bowl and top with mint leaves. (If using peppermint oil take a toothpick and dip it in a bottle of food grade essential oil of peppermint and then swish the toothpick in the soup.

2. As you drink it enjoy the sensory brightness of chewing on the sweet watermelon, the little chunks of ginger, and the mint leaves.

Watermelon Antianxiety Tonic (Makes 5 cups concentrate)

It might sound strange to drink apple cider vinegar, but when combined in this drink it is delicious, refreshing, raises the spirits, quells anxiety, and increases energy. Even children will enjoy this drink. The watermelon is rich in potassium and B vitamins and contains the highest levels of lycopene of all fruits—a powerful antioxidant. The raw apple cider vinegar is acidifying and helps relieve anxiety, depression, hyperventilation, panic, and fatigue. Make a batch and drink 1–2 cups a day for several days.

Ingredients

3 c. water, plus more to serve

¼ tsp. sea salt

¼ c. raw organic honey

6 c. watermelon, coarsely chopped

1 c. tightly packed fresh spearmint

1 c. raw apple cider vinegar

10 drops liquid stevia

Ice cubes

Sliced watermelon, sliced unwaxed organic cucumber, and spearmint, for garnish

Directions

1. Bring the water and the salt to a boil in a medium saucepan. Remove from the heat. Add honey and stir to dissolve.

2. Combine the watermelon and mint in a large bowl. Stir in the honey water and let cool to room temperature. Add the vinegar. Steep the mixture in the refrigerator for several hours or up to overnight.

3. Pour the mixture through a strainer. The watermelon chunks can be eaten, if desired. Pour the juice into a clean glass jar and store in the refrigerator for up to 1 week.

4. Because the juice is very concentrated, pour just ¼ cup of the juice into a glass over ice and dilute with ¾ cup water. Add stevia (or a little honey) to taste.

5. Garnish with the watermelon, cucumber, and mint.

GOOD MOOD ALTERNATIVES TO SUGAR: OVERCOMING THE ADDICTION

If our brain needs glucose and glucose is a type of sugar, why is refined sugar bad for mental health? Sugar that is refined from sugar cane or sugar beets depletes B vitamins and immune-support minerals such as zinc, and it also reduces the body's natural capacity to digest and absorb glucose. Refined sugar is also highly inflammatory; it exacerbates pain and raises triglycerides and cholesterol levels. Its use is a major cause of the worldwide epidemic of type 2 diabetes. Following ancestral diets has been found to be beneficial for the prevention and treatment of diabetes (Korn, 2009). It is surprisingly common for vegetarians, whose diets are carbohydrate heavy and often protein light, to have reactive hypoglycemia and eat a lot of sugar because of their low protein intake. Vegetarians often benefit from increasing the use of eggs and dairy along with vegetables and legumes, ensuring that their protein sources provide the complete source of amino acids, the building blocks of brain chemicals for mood, focus, and stable blood sugar.

Fibers and mucilaginous foods, such as edible cacti and slippery elm bark, slow the absorption of sugars in the intestines. Foods high in water-soluble fiber, like flax seed, apple pectin, and seaweeds, are also highly beneficial at amounts from 80 to 100 grams per day. Research shows that psyllium husk improves glycemic control and fat control, and it reduces cholesterol. However, if you consume these fibers for satiety or constipation, do so at least two hours after you take your nutritional supplements so absorption of nutrients will not be affected.

HOW TO STOP THE SUGAR ADDICTION

Going on a protein-rich diet for 7–10 days can help you withdraw from sugar and refined carbohydrates. Eat small amounts (2–4 ounces) of protein six times a day (about every 3–4 hours) and 1–2 servings of a root vegetable—such as sweet potato or carrots—topped with butter, coconut oil, or olive oil, along with raw salads or cooked green vegetables. Most people will do well ensuring there is at least some, if not abundant amounts of, animal protein included in each meal. There is no need to be hungry, so eat as often as you need to.

Following this change in diet, most people lose their craving for refined carbohydrates and sugars. Afterward, small amounts of additional carbohydrates, such as fruit and grains, can be restored to the diet each day.

Going off sugar does not mean the end of sweet treats. Just transform the treats into brainbow food. One of the best ways to engage children and adults alike in giving up candy is to make candy that is healthy and medicinal for mood. Children love making these treats in the following recipe. Make a double batch, and freeze the extra treats.

Chocolate Almond Coconut Joy (Makes about 30 pieces)

This recipe is good medicine—a delicious and healthy alternative to commercial candy bars. Making these treats can be a group activity and is especially fun to do with children and adolescents, who can learn about healthy "treats" and the effects of sugar on focus and well-being. The anti-inflammatory properties of both coconut and dark chocolate make this treat a healthy and effective mood booster.

Equipment
Two sheets parchment paper
Half-sheet pan

Ingredients

½ c. blue agave, raw honey, or maple syrup; or 20–25 drops of liquid stevia

2 tbsp. butter

2 c. unsweetened shredded coconut, lightly packed

17 oz. organic dark chocolate (no sugar added), chopped or broken into small pieces

30–35 lightly roasted and unsalted almonds

Directions

1. In a saucepan, bring the agave (or other sweetener) to a low boil over medium heat. Add the butter and melt it, stirring occasionally. Once fully integrated, remove from heat and let sit for 2–3 minutes. Add the coconut slowly, stirring until it is fully coated.

2. Put a sheet of the parchment paper on a clean cutting board. Pour the agave-coconut mixture onto the parchment, spreading it with a spatula or the flat side of a knife.

3. Spread the mixture to about ½ inch thickness. Form into a rectangle, roughly 9 by 4 inches, and cover with another piece of parchment. Using a rolling pin or bottle, lightly roll the mixture outward until it is about ¼ inch thick.

4. Allow the mixture to cool slightly, remove the top parchment, then sharp-cut the mixture into strips about 1-inch wide. Working crosswise cut the strips again into 2-inch rectangles. Slide the coconut squares, still on their parchment, onto a half-sheet pan, allowing them to set while you prepare the chocolate. (Tip: Coat your knife with butter to keep the mixture from sticking.)

5. Next, place the chopped or broken chocolate into a heat-proof bowl. Set the bowl over a pan of simmering water, but don't allow the bowl to touch the water. Melt the chocolate, stirring constantly with a rubber spatula, until it is smooth. Remove the melted chocolate from the heat.

6. Place the second piece of parchment paper on the cutting board. Working quickly while the chocolate is still warm, spread a thin layer of the chocolate into a rectangle that is more or less the size of the sheet of coconut squares, using only half of the melted chocolate. When finished, place it in the refrigerator to cool.

7. Remove the coconut squares from the refrigerator and immediately turn them out onto the sheet of melted chocolate. Press down firmly using your hands. Remove the parchment from the coconut. Using a knife, separate the coconut squares following the cuts made earlier.

8. Top each coconut square with a roasted almond. Using a spoon, ladle the rest of the melted chocolate across the coconut squares, creating an even layer. Refrigerate the pan for 20–30 minutes to allow the chocolate to harden. Recut the squares and refrigerate until ready to serve.

Sugar Substitutes

Stevia is the ideal sugar substitute. It is a hundred times sweeter than sugar and has been shown to reduce blood sugar. While the powdered form of stevia can tend to leave a bitter aftertaste, the liquid form does not. Either form can be used in drinks or food preparation.

Stevia / Sugar Conversion		
Sugar amount	Equivalent stevia powdered extract	Equivalent stevia liquid concentrate
1 cup	1 teaspoon	1 teaspoon (24–36 drops)
1 tablespoon	¼ teaspoon	6–9 drops
1 teaspoon	A pinch to ¹⁄₁₆ teaspoon	2–4 drops

COOKING WITH SPICES AND HERBS

Here are some savvy herbs and spices for cooking:
- Ginger
- Saffron
- Turmeric
- Garlic
- Basil
- Oregano
- Sea Salt

Herbs and spices are sources of nutrients, medicine, and culinary pleasure for the brain and mind. Some spices, like basil and oregano, are best used when fresh, but others like cardamom and cinnamon are available only in dry form. Ginger has anti-inflammatory and antioxidant effects, relieving pain and spasms—including menstrual cramps—as well as relieving nausea. Saffron, which has antidepressant effects, is commonly added to rice while it is cooking. Turmeric root, which may help to prevent Alzheimer's and Parkinson's disease, reduces headache pain and supports liver, gallbladder, and digestive health by stimulating bile flow. Try adding turmeric to curries, stir-fries, and sauces. Turmeric and its anti-inflammatory chemical *curcumin* require black pepper in order to work, so make sure you add whole peppercorns to your dishes when using fresh turmeric root. It is wise to not overdo the use of any spice or herb but to use in moderation and to rotate your use of spices. There may also be specific reasons why some culinary herbs and spices are not appropriate for you to take at medicinal levels. For example, pregnant women and people at risk of kidney stones should avoid large amounts of turmeric. Black pepper must not be consumed in excess of 1 teaspoon a day when the cardiac stimulant digoxin or the anticonvulsant phenytoin are used.

Freeze fresh herbs by chopping them up. If you can get a lot of fresh basil during the summer, make pesto and freeze it for the winter months. Plan your meals each week that will use up the herb you want to buy that week so that it does not go to waste. Dried herbs should be stored in a cool, dry place in tightly sealed containers. You can get creative, making your own spice mixes, and substituting one herb for another in recipes.

Mental Health Benefits of Herbs and Spices			
Name	Form	Use	Benefits
Basil	Fresh, dried, or capsules	Mediterranean and Italian dishes, pasta, sauces, dressings, and pesto	Antioxidant Protects against free radical damage, reduces inflammation Good source of magnesium, vitamin K, and manganese Holy basil, known as *tulsi*, is anti-inflammatory, antioxidant, and adaptogenic
Black pepper	Whole or ground	Slightly spicy seasoning for all kinds of foods	Increases hydrochloric acid production in the stomach and improves digestion Required for absorption of curcumin (turmeric)

Cardamom	Ground, seeds, or pods	Tea and coffee, curry, grain dishes, meat dishes, or with winter squash	Analgesic Good source of calcium, sulfur, and phosphorus Improves digestion and relieves gastrointestinal problems Tea reduces stress and depression
Cayenne pepper	Fresh, dried, and ground	Many dishes from around the world, hot sauces, marinades, or used topically	High in vitamin A, B6, C, E, as well as riboflavin, potassium, and manganese Promotes healthy liver function and aids digestion Helpful in migraines, heartburn, and allergies Pain reduction (topical)
Cinnamon	Cinnamon sticks or powder, or as an extract	Breads, meats, soups, hot and cold cereal, drinks, and sweets	Aids digestion and stimulates appetite Rich in manganese and antioxidants Candida treatment Increases glucose uptake Lowers serum glucose in diabetic patients
Cumin	Seeds and ground	Soups, stews, curries, meat dishes, and pickles	Aids digestion and stimulates appetite
Dill	Fresh and dried	Russian, European, Italian, Greek, and African foods; fish, salad dressings, borscht, soups, potatoes, and pickles	Antioxidant Relieves gas Provides vitamin A Antibacterial
Garlic	Fresh, dried, crushed, and capsules	Stir-fries, pastas, marinades, vegetables, meats, dressings, sauces	Improves immunity, lowers blood sugar, and reduces cholesterol and triglyceride levels Antidepressant and anti-inflammatory

Ginger	Tea, fresh or dried, powdered, and liquid extracts	Stir-fries, Asian food, marinades, desserts	Anti-inflammatory and pain relief Relieves gastrointestinal disorders Boosts immune system Relieves nausea
Oregano	Dried or fresh	Mediterranean and Italian food; savory and/or spicy dishes; marinades, roasted vegetables, casseroles, pasta sauces, and pizza	Rich in vitamin K Antioxidant Relieves gastrointestinal problems and headaches
Rosemary	Fresh or dried	Mediterranean and Italian cuisine; roasted meats, stuffing, roasted vegetables, soups, stews, marinades, and sauces	Provides vitamin A Anti-inflammatory Aids digestion, relieves gas and headaches, and improves concentration Calming
Tarragon	Fresh and dried	French cuisine; salad dressings, fish, and eggs	Antioxidant Rich in vitamins A and C, and B vitamins Provides calcium, manganese, iron, copper, magnesium, potassium, and zinc Stimulates appetite and aids in anorexia Relieves insomnia
Turmeric	Tea, fresh or powdered form, and liquid extracts	Indian food; curry, stir-fries, sauces	Antioxidant Anti-inflammatory and adaptogenic Relieves pain and depression Improves liver and gallbladder function

Sea Salt

Sea salt is an important culinary medicine to reduce stress and depression, and to increase energy. Unrefined sea salt contains minerals that support adrenal function and other needs of the body—including iron, magnesium, potassium, calcium, manganese, zinc, and iodine.

Try the various colored salts that are available: the gray sea salt, which comes in a larger crystal form or granules; Celtic sea salt; or Himalayan pink salt. These high-quality salts also provide chloride, which helps the body produce hydrochloric acid and improves digestion. Celtic sea salt helps to mineralize and hydrate the body while restoring the sodium-potassium balance. As an alternative to salt, many types of seaweed can be used in soups or with beans.

FERMENTED FOODS

Fermented foods are essential for everyone—but especially for people with anxiety—as they enhance gut function. Fermented foods are a very inexpensive form of essential brain nutrition. Fermenting foods "predigest" the nutrients, and they are rich in enzymes, healthy bacteria, and vitamins. Every culture ferments some kind of food. Explore your own cultural traditions of fermented foods, as well as those of other cultures.

Some fermented foods for your diet	Main ingredients	Geographic origin
Fresh raw sauerkraut	Cabbage	Eastern Europe
Kimchi	Cabbage and spices	Korea
Yogurt	Milk	Caucasus mountains
Kefir	Milk	Caucasus mountains
Miso, natto, and tamari	Soybeans	Japan, China
Kombucha	Black tea	Russia

Miso Soup

Miso soup is a taste worth acquiring. Good quality miso is fresh and kept refrigerated. It is my "go to" soup with any type of digestive upset or illness. Easy to digest and warming, it helps to restore gut bacteria. It is important not to boil the miso, in order to preserve the bacteria. Miso can be made from soybeans or from grains like barley and rice. I recommend a white miso to start, because it is the mildest miso, and you can obtain benefits from it easily.

Ingredients

6 c. of water

¼ c. dried wakame or hijiki seaweed

4 shiitake mushrooms, fresh or dried, sliced thin

4 tbsp. white miso

2 scallions, sliced (for garnish)

1–2 tbsp. of natto, optional

Directions

Soak the seaweed in warm water for 30 minutes prior to cooking.

1. Bring the water to a simmer in a small pot and add the mushrooms and the seaweed. Simmer for 10 minutes. Reduce the heat to low.

2. In a separate bowl, mix together the sweet white miso, adding as much of the hot water as it takes to make a smooth creamy paste. (Add natto, if desired.) Place this mixture into the soup pot and let it heat on low while stirring to dissolve the paste.

3. Serve immediately. Garnish with scallions.

Garlic Yogurt Salad Dressing

This dressing can be made in advance, stored for several days, and used on salads or as a dip for raw vegetables.

Ingredients

¾ c. plain, cow or goat milk yogurt

1 small garlic clove, minced

¼ tsp. dried basil

½ tbsp. apple cider vinegar

¹⁄₁₆ tsp. stevia powder

1 tsp. chopped fresh parsley

4 tbsp. organic mayonnaise

Directions

Whisk all ingredients together in a bowl and serve.

Kimchi

Ingredients

2 heads of napa cabbage, shredded in a food processor

5–10 scallions, finely chopped

2–3 cloves garlic, crushed

1 tsp. fresh ginger, crushed

2 jalapeños, finely minced

2 tbsp. crushed fresh red chili pepper

Half an onion, chopped (optional)

Filtered or distilled water, as needed

½ tsp. Celtic sea salt or Himalayan pink salt

2 tbsp. raw honey

Directions

1. Mix together all ingredients (except water, salt, and honey) in a bowl.

2. Add several cups of the mixture to a blender with filtered or distilled water, the sea salt, and the honey, and blend to make a brine (should be a thick liquid). Starter cultures can be added to the brine if desired.

3. Add remaining chopped vegetables and brine to a 1½-quart glass or stainless steel jar, packing them in snuggly, leaving 2 inches at the top. Take several cabbage leaves, roll them up, and place them at the top to fill this 2-inch space.

4. Let the jar sit for a minimum of 3 days at room temperature. It is best to let them sit for a week or more. The culture should be kept at around 70 degrees F.

MISO SALAD DRESSING

Ingredients

1 tbsp. unseasoned rice vinegar

1 tbsp. white miso

2 tsp. grated peeled fresh ginger

1 garlic clove, minced

½ tsp. honey, or 10 drops stevia liquid (optional)

Pinch of ground black pepper

3 tbsp. sesame or olive oil

Dried red chili pepper flakes, to taste (optional)

Directions

Combine all ingredients; whisk and pour over greens.

Apple Cider Vinegar

Apple cider vinegar is especially good for anxiety and depression. It can be added to salad dressings, or drunk as a beverage each morning with water and a little raw honey. A cup can also be added to the bathtub during a long soak to decrease fatigue. Always use raw, organic, unfiltered, and unpasteurized vinegar that has been naturally brewed, and avoid distilled vinegar which no longer has the natural enzymes, minerals, and nutrients. Mix a teaspoon of apple cider vinegar with water and sip throughout the day to boost energy and balance the pH of the body.

JUICING

Juicing vegetables and fruits is a delicious way to intensify their nutritional benefits. Juicing should be considered as culinary medicine, not as a beverage. Fresh juices are potent forms of vitamins that can be used for specific purposes. However, juices are missing fiber and should be balanced with whole fruits and vegetables. Juices are an easy way to incorporate chlorophyll-rich vegetables into the diet, for adults as well as children. Since many fruits are high in fructose, people with sugar handling-problems such as pre-diabetes or diabetes should be careful about the amount of fruit juice they drink in one setting.

Juice cleanses incorporate the use of fresh vegetable juice for a short period of time, usually 1–3 days. They are used to improve health and to treat specific conditions, and they should be done under the supervision of your health care provider. Carrot and green juice, and other vegetable juices, can be used in small quantities daily rather than for strict cleanses, providing much of the same benefit. The following is an ideal juice to begin with:

Carrot Juice Jubilee (Serves 2)

Ingredients

1 lb. organic carrots

1 organic beet

1 organic apple

Small piece of fresh ginger

1 tsp. coconut oil (optional)

Directions

1. Wash and cut all the vegetables and fruits so they can pass through the juicer, keeping the skin intact.
2. Strain the juice lightly, keeping some of the pulp.

Green Juices

Juice is an easy way to obtain high density nutrients from greens, celery, cucumbers, parsley, cilantro, and other fresh green foods. To adjust to the flavor of green juices, try starting with milder vegetables like cucumbers and celery and slowly work up to cabbage, spinach, and lettuce. Bitter greens—like kale, dandelion, and mustard greens—can be added in small amounts. One-half to one whole lime or lemon can be added to cut bitter flavors, or you can use carrot juice as the base. Other flavor enhancers include cranberries and fresh ginger. Use organic vegetables, and always drink juices right after making them to get the most benefit.

Here are some ingredients you can use for savvy green juices:
- Cucumber
- Celery
- Kale
- Dandelion
- Mustard greens
- Parsley
- Cilantro
- Cabbage
- Spinach

COFFEE

Coffee is a drug, not a beverage. So use it wisely.

Coffee, a favorite beverage in our culture, enhances mood, stimulates alertness, and increases mental performance. When used in moderation (1–2 cups early in the day), coffee can improve mood and focus, but when used in excess it has negative side effects such as anxiety and insomnia. Espresso has less caffeine than drip coffee. People with anxiety or panic should avoid coffee; however, people who are depressed, have ADHD, or need cognitive support may benefit from moderate use of coffee.

Cold-Brewed Coffee

People who have GERD do best without coffee or by using cold-brewed coffee, which reduces the acids significantly.

Ingredients

Organic coffee, coarsely ground

Directions

1. Start with coarsely ground, organic coffee. If you are grinding your beans at the store, use the "French press" setting.
2. Combine ⅓ cup of grounds with 1½ cups of water in a glass container at room temperature. Stir well.
3. Cover the container and let steep in a cool, dark place for 12–16 hours.
4. Strain the mixture using a coffee filter. This is a concentrated coffee extract and should be mixed with water to taste.
5. To make iced coffee, mix equal parts coffee extract with cold water and add ice.
6. To make hot coffee, use equal parts coffee extract (at room temperature) and boiling water. These ratios can be adjusted depending on how strong you like your coffee.
7. Use the coffee concentrate within 1–2 weeks.

Brain Butter Coffee

This combination of cold-brewed coffee, raw butter, organic coconut fat, and almond milk is a pure cognition and energy medicine. This energizing drink sustains you for many more hours than coffee alone and is delicious. The concept of combining fat and caffeine (from tea) originates with indigenous people of Tibet. This drink may be enjoyed by everyone, but it is especially good for slow metabolizers who are not hungry in the morning and yet need sustaining fuel for the brain and body until the first meal of the day.

Ingredients

4 oz. of cold-brewed coffee

1–2 tsp. of raw organic butter

1 tsp. coconut fat

2 oz. of almond milk

stevia to taste (optional)

Directions

1. Heat the cold-brewed coffee in a small saucepan.
2. Add the almond milk so the mixture is warm to hot (however you like it best)—but do *not* bring it to a boil.
3. Transfer the mixture to a blender, add the butter and oil, and blend it until it is well mixed and frothy. (Another option is to use an immersion blender or frother, add the butter and oil to the saucepan directly, and froth until well blended. Make sure that you do *not* cook the fat or boil the coffee.)
4. Pour and enjoy your brain butter coffee.

The following table lists various beverages you can substitute for coffee.

Coffee Substitutes		
Beverage	Caffeine or not	Ingredients
Inka	No	Roasted barley, rye, chicory and beet roots
Roastaroma	No	Roasted barley, roasted chicory, roasted carob, cinnamon, allspice, and Chinese star anise. (contains gluten)
Teeccino	No	Carob, barley, chicory, almonds, dates, figs, coffee flavor
Roasted dandelion root	No	Roasted dandelion root
Dark roast yerba mate	Yes	Roasted yerba mate
Chai	Yes	Black tea, cardamom, cloves, cinnamon, ginger
Genmaicha	Yes	Green tea and roasted brown rice

Caffeine is medicine for some, not for others. If you feel you will do better without caffeine, or perhaps with not as much, try this approach to withdrawal:

How to Kick the Caffeine Habit

1. During the first week—using only organic coffee—brew ¾ regular coffee to ¼ decaf coffee.
2. During the second week, reduce the ratio to ½ regular coffee and ½ decaf.
3. During the third week, brew just ¼ regular coffee and ¾ decaf.
4. Finally, transition to completely decaf coffee, and you are caffeine-free!

TEAS

Teas make a great alternative to coffee and are also rich in antioxidants and mood boosters due to the caffeine.

Green Tea

Green tea (*Camellia sinensis*) is a traditional beverage in Asian societies and is known for its calming effects. Green tea contains the relaxation amino acid L-theanine that counteracts the effects of the caffeine. Green tea is beneficial for cognitive health, memory, and attention. Add a teaspoon of green tea powder to a smoothie daily to support cognitive function. A special form of green tea made from the entire leaf is called *matcha* and comes in powder form. It can be added to a smoothie or whisked together with steamed milk.

TURMERIC-ROOIBOS BRAIN CHAI

This tea makes a delicious mood refresher with or without the caffeine from the black tea.

Makes 4 servings.

Ingredients

5 c. water

2-in. piece of fresh ginger, coarsely chopped

2-in. piece of fresh turmeric, coarsely chopped

1 tbsp. cardamom pods

1 tsp. cloves

½ tsp. black peppercorns

1 cinnamon stick

1–2 tbsp. rooibos (red bush) tea, to taste

1 c. milk (coconut, almond, rice, etc.)

1 tsp. vanilla extract

1 tsp. extra-virgin coconut oil

Sweetener of choice (honey, stevia, or agave)

Organic black tea, loose or bag (optional for caffeine)

Directions

1. Place the water, ginger, and turmeric in a medium size pot and bring to a boil. Reduce heat to medium and simmer for 5 minutes. Add the cardamom pods, cloves, black peppercorns, and cinnamon, and simmer for another 15 minutes.

2. Strain the liquid into a large bowl, reserving the spices and roots to use for another batch of chai. Add the rooibos tea to the bowl (and the optional black tea) and cover, steeping for 5–10 minutes.

3. Strain the tea back into the pot. Add the milk, vanilla, and coconut oil, and gently heat at medium-low for 5 minutes, stirring to combine. Serve in individual cups and sweeten to taste using honey, stevia, or agave nectar.

CHAPTER 10

Putting It All Together: Mood-Savvy Vitamins and Special Nutrients

A healthy diet is essential for mental health; however, it is not generally sufficient by itself to treat mental illness. Vitamins, minerals, amino acids, special nutrients, and glandulars are also necessary to alter the biochemistry of our brain, mind, and body. Although some of them are contained in foods, many are more effectively utilized as supplements. These supplements are essential to restoring mental wellness and reducing or eliminating psychotropic medications.

"Can I get all the vitamins and minerals I need from eating food?" is a question I often hear. There is no simple answer to that question. To prevent or treat an illness, I am convinced the most beneficial approach is to take vitamins, minerals, and nutrients in addition to a selection of healthy, whole foods. In the pages that follow you will find simple nutrient combinations designed to treat specific conditions along with general dosing recommendations and protocols. The effective use of these resources, however, depends upon an individualized approach.

Nutritional therapy for mental health is best accomplished in collaboration with a clinician. Before beginning any nutrient program, consult with your nutritional therapist or clinician to identify possible interactions with your current medication regimen and with any diseases for which you are currently receiving treatment. Remember that dosing should be adjusted according to age and body weight, so the suggested protocols in this book are approximate.

Many people choose to explore the use of diet and nutritional supplementation in order to stay off or get off pharmaceutical medications. The pioneering physician and scientist Carl Pfeiffer said "For every drug that benefits a patient, there is a natural substance that can achieve the same effect." This is the philosophy behind using nutrient resources for bringing balance and wellness to the brain, mind, and body. To withdraw from and eliminate psychotropics, you can benefit from combining a full-spectrum approach that includes nutrient-dense foods and nutritional supplements to ease withdrawal and address the underlying needs of the brain and body. I encourage you to work with your nutritional therapist, as well as your prescriber, using my clinical textbook *Nutrition Essentials for Mental Health* (Korn, 2016), which provides more detailed information on dosing, indications, and contraindications.

HOW TO TAKE NUTRITIONAL SUPPLEMENTS

Most vitamins and minerals should be taken with food, preferably when at least half the meal has been eaten. The exceptions are amino acids to support the brain, and proteolytic enzymes when used to reduce inflammation. These should be taken on an empty stomach.

It is important to take a break from all nutrients for 5 days each month to give the body, brain, and mind a rest.

Mood Smoothie

Smoothies are an easy way to ingest nutrients and oils as an alternative to taking pills and capsules. Capsules can be opened and pills can be ground in a mortar and pestle or in a small electric grinder. Experiment with ratios and quantities as well as with fruits and base liquids. Make flavored ice cubes for smoothies in advance; for example freeze coconut milk or water, green tea, chamomile tea, or pomegranate juice.

For a simple meal or when digestion is impaired, add whey or hemp protein powder as an easily digested source of protein; however, ensure that it is made without sugar or additives.

Ingredients

4 oz. plain almond, hemp, or goat milk yogurt
2 tsp. liquid fish oil (2,000 mg of omega-3 fatty acids)

¼ frozen banana (peel banana and place in freezer ahead of time)

¼ c. frozen raspberries, blueberries, mangos, or fruit of choice

3–10 drops liquid stevia (optional, to taste)

½ tsp. green tea powder or 2 green tea ice cubes

Powdered nutrients

Powdered whey protein (optional)

Directions

1. Place ingredients in a blender.
2. Add enough water and ice cubes for either a thin drink or a thick frozen shake.
3. Blend to desired consistency, pour into a glass, and enjoy!

TIPS FOR ORGANIZING NUTRITIONAL SUPPLEMENTS

1. Organize enough pills for 3–4 weeks at a time.
2. Place your nutrient bottles in a row.
3. In front of the bottles, place the same number of paper cupcake cups as bottles in a row.
4. Make as many rows as there are times of day. For example, if you take nutrients three times a day, make three rows of cups. Now you have three rows of cupcake cups: one row for breakfast, one row for lunch, and one for dinner that are 10 cups long.
5. Open one bottle at a time and put one capsule/pill into each cup until each cup is full for that time of day the capsule is called for.
6. Go through each bottle until you have completed all of them. You now have cups filled for a month.
7. Obtain small plastic bags and begin to fill a bag one cup at a time and put elastics around one each of your breakfast, lunch, and dinner bags so you end up with 30 packs of bags that will be ready each day.
8. If you will be at the office or on the road, place an extra bag where you might need it.
9. Keep them cool and dry and out of the sun.
10. If you do not like pills or capsules, you can grind pills in a food grinder and turn them to powder, adding it to smoothies.
11. Search out liquid or emulsified supplement options.

VITAMINS

Vitamins are divided into *water-soluble* and *fat-soluble* vitamins. Water-soluble means that they can be dissolved in water and are not stored in the body. The risk of overdosing with water-soluble vitamins is very low. Fat-soluble means they are absorbed by fat and require sufficient dietary fats to be of use; they are stored in body tissues and thus can be overdosed more easily, though this is rare. Vitamins work synergistically.

B-Complex Vitamins

B-complex vitamins are essential for brain and nervous system function.

Special B Vitamins

In addition to the B-complex vitamins—which contain all 8 B vitamins and are therefore of particular importance—you may take any of the individual B vitamins to increase the dose of only that B vitamin:

B_1 **(thiamine):** Take 5–40 mg/day. Found in beans, blackstrap molasses, brewer's yeast, fish, lentils, nuts, organ meats, pork, and rice. Helps to prevent Alzheimer's, regulates the nervous system, assists with energy metabolism, boosts immunity, and is especially useful for people who are fatigued due to chronically low blood pressure.

B_3 **(niacinamide):** Take 500 mg/day (anxiety and fatigue); 1,000–4,500 mg/day (schizophrenia); 500 mg 3 times/day (depression); 1,500–18,000 mg/day (alcohol recovery).

B_5 **(pantothenic acid):** Take 500 mg/day. Found in avocado, broccoli, cauliflower, chicken, eggs, lentils, meat, mushrooms (shiitake and cremini), sweet potato, turkey, vegetables, and yogurt. Reduces depression; balances blood sugar; aids sleep, fatigue, and insomnia; lifts mood; and aids neurotransmitter synthesis.

B_6 **(pyridoxal 5'–phosphate):** Take: 50–100 mg daily. Found in sunflower seeds, pistachio nuts, tuna, turkey, pork, prunes, bananas, avocadoes spinach, black beans, blackstrap molasses, brown rice, cantaloupe, chicken, cod, collard greens, beef, flax seeds, garlic, red bell peppers, salmon, snapper, spinach, strawberries, and turnip greens.

B$_7$ (biotin) (also called Vitamin H): Take 500–2,000 mcg/day. Found in organ meats, (esp. liver), red meat, seafood, eggs, almonds, avocado, bananas, nuts, nut butters, berries, sardines, and chard. Supports adrenal function, synthesizes fatty acids and amino acids, and supports nerve health.

B$_8$ (inositol): Take 5–20 grams/day in divided doses for obsessive compulsive disorder. Found in fresh green beans, artichokes, okra, eggplant, cantaloupe, and citrus fruits. Supports neurological function, and improves and balances mood.

B$_9$ (folic acid): Take 15 mg L-methylfolate, combined with methyl B-12 and niacin daily for major depression. (Do not use folic acid supplements—use L-methylfolate.) Found in asparagus, avocado, beef liver, beets, brewer's yeast, brussels sprouts, grains, leafy greens, beans, orange juice, root vegetables, salmon, spinach, turnips, and whole grains. Supports proper nervous system functioning; improves mood disorders, depression, and bipolar disorder.

B$_{12}$ methylcobalamin: Take 1,000–2,000 mcg/day. Found in beef liver, shellfish (clams, shrimp, scallops), cod, dairy (esp. yogurt), eggs, fish, salmon, sardines, tuna, and animal protein like red meat. Boosts mood and provides cognitive support in elders; it is a required supplement for vegetarians.

MINERALS

Minerals are the "sparkplugs" (Watts, 2006) of the body. They support the transformation of food into nutrients that can be assimilated by the body. A lack or imbalance of minerals can be as detrimental as an excess. Because minerals work together synergistically, it is important to first do a "tissue mineral analysis" to identify bio-individual needs for mineral supplementation.

The next step is to take a balanced mineral supplement that includes easily absorbed minerals that match your health needs. Look for a well-balanced supplement that has a range of minerals. Among the most important minerals to supplement mental health—<u>in addition</u> to a multimineral complex—are chromium, lithium, magnesium, selenium, and zinc.

The following minerals are essential to include in your good mood diet:

Calcium: Found in dairy products, spinach, bone broth, and dark greens combined with vinegar. Helps the nervous system communicate, and can ameliorate irritability, anxiety, and depression (but taking too much can increase depression).

CALCIUM-RICH SOUP

Calcium can be absorbed when obtained from calcium-rich food. Too often we think children (and the elderly) need milk for calcium, but cow milk is best avoided. Therefore, this recipe is an ideal way to obtain calcium, and it takes only about 10 minutes to prepare for the Crock-Pot. Throw the following ingredients into the Crock-Pot early in the morning and by evening you have a nourishing soup enjoyed by children and adults alike:

Ingredients

8 c. of bone broth (and a marrow bone if you have it)

2 c. of dry pinto beans

3 tbsp. of blackstrap molasses

1 head of chopped broccoli including stems

4 potatoes, cubed

1 bunch of kale, chopped

1 pinch of your favorite seaweed

Directions

1. Cook on low for 8 hours.
2. Add a pinch of sea salt and black pepper before serving. You can top it with walnuts.

Chromium: For hypoglycemia and mood regulation, take 200 mcg 3 times/day; for binge eating disorder and depression, take 600–1,000 mcg 3 times/day. Found in brewer's yeast, liver, mushrooms, and whole grains. Helps regulate blood sugar levels, improves mood, and reduces carbohydrate cravings.

Copper: Should only be supplemented with a professional's advice. Found in seafood (esp. oysters and lobster), kale, avocado, asparagus, chocolate, grains, molasses, mushrooms, nuts, sesame seeds, tahini, and nuts. Excess tissue copper is common due to well water, soil, or pesticide exposures and is found especially in vegetarians or people under chronic stress. Excess copper may contribute to fatigue, premenstrual syndrome, anorexia, depression, anxiety, allergies, autism, schizophrenia, and postpartum depression.

Iodine: Found in eggs, sea vegetables, iodized salt, fish, shellfish, and strawberries. Promotes production of thyroid hormones. Lack of iodine can contribute to hypothyroid depression and cognitive decline.

Iron: Best obtained from foods such as beef and beef liver, chicken and chicken liver, clams, halibut, mussels, oysters, sardines, turkey, lentils, spinach, beans, pumpkin seeds, and sesame seeds. Iron boosts immunity and reduces fatigue.

Lithium (orotate): For brain antiaging, take 10–20 mg/day; for PTSD and traumatic brain injury (TBI), take 50–150 mg/day of lithium orotate. Lithium is one of the most important minerals for supplementation. Also found in some mineral waters, sugarcane, seaweed, lemons, and eggs.

Magnesium: Take 200–1,200 mg/day, or to bowel tolerance. Found in almonds, avocado, black beans, cashews, fortified foods, legumes, oatmeal, nuts, peanuts, seeds, spinach, whole grains, and yogurt. Promotes healthy blood sugar and blood pressure levels, reduces oxidative stress and inflammation, relaxes muscles, and aids sleep. **Note:** Taking too much supplemental magnesium can increase depression and fatigue, especially in natural carnivores.

EPSOM SALTS BATH

Epsom salts (magnesium sulfate) baths are a simple way to absorb magnesium, relax muscles, reduce anxiety, and prepare for sleep. Add 1 cup of Epsom salts (magnesium sulfate) to a warm/hot bath and soak for 20 minutes. This bath can be completed 1 hour before bed or can be taken as a foot soak if there is no bathing facility.

Potassium (orotate): Take 99 mg/day. Found in bananas, beets and beet greens, blackstrap molasses, carrots, clams, cod, halibut, prunes, turkey, salmon, spinach, sweet potatoes, tomatoes, tuna, winter squash, and yogurt. Necessary for electrical conductivity of the brain and nerves. Delivers oxygen and transports serotonin in the brain; improves cognitive function; ameliorates depression, anorexia, insomnia, mental fatigue, anxiety, mood swings, psychosis, nervous system disorders, and confusion.

Selenium: Take 100–200 mcg/day as a complex of 3 types of selenium, preferably combined with vitamin E. Found in sardines (and fish skins), garlic, onions, bananas, prunes, turkey, beets, spinach, salmon, organ meats, grains, Brazil nuts, raw dairy products, eggs, and meat. Elevates mood, supports normal thyroid function, and prevents cognitive decline and brain aging.

Zinc: Take 25 mg 2–3 times/day. Found in beef, cashews, garbanzo beans, grains, lamb, lentils, nuts, oysters, poultry, pumpkin seeds, quinoa, sesame seeds, shrimp, and turkey. Promotes immune function and insulin production. Anti-inflammatory, antidepressant, and antioxidant. Digestive aid useful in depression, autism, schizophrenia, impaired memory, ADHD, and binge eating disorder (bulimia/purging).

AMINO ACIDS

Amino acids are the building blocks of proteins and neurotransmitters. Utilizing amino acid therapies can contribute to an overall plan to prevent, reduce, or eliminate psychotropic pharmaceutical medications.

Modes of Administration

Amino acids are delivered to the body through the proteins in food as well as through capsules, powders, and intravenous therapy. When possible, take amino acids 30 minutes away from a meal so they will not compete with the amino acids in food. Determining the best dose of amino acids should be done in conjunction with a health professional to ensure finding the correct balance of amino acids.

Amino acids are available in powder or liquid form and can be added to water or a smoothie. There are special amino acid combinations available in liquid drops that are designed for maintaining blood sugar and mood during the day. I suggest that children and adults with ADHD, hypoglycemia, or adrenal stress carry a small dropper bottle and take 10–30 drops under the tongue during the day if they feel their energy, mood, or focus drop—until they can eat some food.

Start Here: Free Amino Acid Therapy

The use of amino acid therapy is an essential component of mood regulation. People with mood swings, anxiety, fADHD, and memory/cognitive concerns will all benefit from a free amino acid blend. Nearly everyone will benefit from a supplement that has free amino acids as the foundation for neurotransmitter function. Amino acids should be delivered by increasing all the amino acids in the form of free amino acids. This prevents increasing one at the expense of another. Too often people make the mistake of taking 5-hydroxytryptophan (5-HTP) or a GABA precursor alone, but most people require support for all amino acids. Once all the amino acids are provided, additional amounts of single amino acids can be delivered as necessary.

Contraindications: People with tardive dyskinesia should not take phenylalanine supplements. Kidney or liver disease patients should consult their primary care practitioner before taking high amounts of amino acids.

Foods and Nutrients that Support Specific Neurotransmitters

The following table identifies the foods and nutrients that provide specific amino acid support for the neurotransmitters that affect brain chemistry.

Amino acids/nutrients	Foods	Neurotransmitters
Glutamine, taurine, milk-derived neuropeptides, lithium orotate, phenibut	Walnuts, oats, spinach, beans, liver, mackerel	GABA
Tryptophan, 5-HTP, B vitamins—especially B_{12}, B_6, niacinamide, folic acid	Salmon, beef, lamb, figs, bananas, root vegetables, brown rice	Serotonin
Tyrosine, DL-phenylalanine, B_{12}, B_6	Coffee, tea, eggs, pork, dark chocolate, ricotta cheese	Dopamine

Tyrosine	Meats, fish, cheese	Norepinephrine
GPC choline, phosphatidylserine, acetyl-L-carnitine, huperzine A	Eggs, liver, salmon, shrimp, nut butters, coffee	Acetylcholine
Glutamic acid	Caffeine, fermented foods, chicken, eggs, dairy	Glutamate
Bioactive milk peptides	Casein (milk), gluten (grains), spinach, fat, fasting	Endogenous opioids
Fish oil, lactobacilli	Hemp seeds/hemp oil	Cannabinoids

GLANDULARS

Glandulars provide some of the most potent nutritional therapies available and should be part of every mental health nutritional protocol. Using glandulars is like refurbishing parts on your car that have worn down or no longer function efficiently. Glandulars are the "replacement parts" that we need to aid our organs and glands.

The use of fresh and dried animal glands as nutritional therapy has a long history. Our ancestors, and the indigenous peoples who hunt for food today, considered the glands among the most prized and medicinal parts of an animal. Organ meats and glands are more nutritious than muscle meats, and until modern practices started to eliminate access to these glands and organs, they were considered most important. Glands were an extensive part of the medical repertoire until recently, when synthetic hormones were developed, yet we see vestiges of the use of glandulars even today in medicine, like the use of porcine thyroid glandular for hypothyroidism. While glands and organs in the form of whole food are healthy, you cannot always obtain them, nor eat a sufficient amount to provide medicinal benefit when you are ill—this is when the use of freeze-dried (lyophilized) glandulars and organs is required.

Here is a list of savvy glandulars for mental health:
- Adrenal—Helps the body respond to stress and reduces fatigue.
- Brain—Addresses cognitive function, response to stress and depression, and PTSD.

- Hypothalamus–Helps the body/mind respond to stress, helps regulate sleep-wake cycle.
- Liver–Detoxifies, aids drug and alcohol recovery.
- Pancreas–Supports fat digestion, blood glucose levels, and immune function.
- Thymus–Supports immune function affected by stress.
- Thyroid–Supports low thyroid function.

ESSENTIAL FATTY ACIDS

Generous use of essential fatty acids supports brain structure and synaptic communication. Higher blood levels of fish oil are associated with increased brain volume. Fish oils are also used for the treatment of traumatic brain injury.

The following fatty acids are essential components of a good mood diet:

- Fish oils support learning ability and play an important role in brain development and growth. They are anti-inflammatory; aid cognitive performance and memory; help depression, PTSD, bipolar disorder, and ADHD; and may reduce psychotic symptoms. Cod liver oil in the form of fermented oil is a superior source of vitamins A and D.
- Flax seed oil supports healthy cholesterol levels and balanced blood glucose levels, and it may be helpful in autoimmune diseases.
- Black currant seed oil, borage oil, and evening primrose oil help to reduce depression. They are anti-inflammatory, and they are especially good to combine with fish oil for anxiety, skin-related problems, and alcohol recovery. They regulate hormones and boost nerve transmission.

VITAMINS A, D, E, AND K

One of your best choices is to take the fat-soluble vitamins A, D, E and K with fish oil and/or black current oil, borage oil, or evening primrose oil when you eat a fat-rich meal. *ADEK* is an acronym for the fat-soluble vitamins A, D, E, and K, which are described as follows:

A (beta-carotene form): Take 10,000–25,000 IU/day and eat sweet potatoes, carrots, (raw) dark leafy greens, apricots, butternut squash, red peppers, eggs, peas, parsley, and beef liver. Boosts immunity and is good for lung health. There is some evidence that it improves mood as well.

D: Take 2,000 IU/day, up to 50,000/week for short term. Found in eggs, sardines, salmon, and tuna. Vitamin D is essential to reduce pain and depression, and to boost immunity.

E (full spectrum tocopherols and tocotrienols): Vitamin E refers to a group of compounds that contain alpha, beta gamma and delta prefixes to tocopherols and tocotrienols and a Vitamin E supplement should designate that it contains all of these types. Take 400 IU/day, and eat almonds, spinach, asparagus, beet greens, avocado, Swiss chard, and sunflower seeds. Improves blood flow, and decreases brain inflammation; antidepressant.

K (K_1 and K_2): Take 2,000 mcg/day. Eat broccoli, brussels sprouts, cauliflower, dairy, miso, leafy greens, liver, meat, eggs, and drink green tea. Anti-inflammatory, antidepressant, and protects against cognitive decline, slowing the progression of Alzheimer's.

All these fat-soluble vitamins can be found in emulsified droplet form or in small capsules, making them easy to take daily.

CORE 6 SUPPLEMENT PROGRAM

The core supplement program combines the following six types of nutritional supplements to get you started with the basics and to support your savvy food choices:

1. Vitamins
2. Minerals
3. Amino acids
4. Glandulars
5. Fats
6. Special nutrients

In the Resources section at the end of the book, I provide recommendations for my favorite high-quality sources of these brain-savvy nutrients.

Most adults will benefit from a core supplement program that contains the following (Note that children under 15 should avoid glandulars.):

- B-complex vitamins
- Multimineral complex
- Vitamins A,D E and K
- Free amino acids
- Fish oil
- Probiotics
- Glandulars (adrenal or hypothalamus)

SPECIAL NUTRIENTS AND SUPPLEMENTS

To augment the core 6 program, add any of the following supplements that are relevant to your individual symptoms:

Theanine: An amino acid found in both green and black tea. It crosses the blood-brain barrier, where it acts as an anxiolytic—to reduce anxiety. Improves learning and memory, and provides a sense of energized relaxation.

Lactium (bioactive milk peptides): Developed in France, lactium is the generic name of bioactive milk peptides—amino acid chains concentrated from casein (derived from cow milk) that act on GABA receptors. Lactium reduces stress, improves sleep, and is a gentle and effective alternative to medication for anxiety and insomnia.

Melatonin: A hormone synthesized as the final metabolite by the tryptophan-serotonin pathway. Can be used for sleep or to reregulate circadian rhythm due to jet lag. Melatonin should always be used with caution, and as a small part of an overall plan for improving sleep, using a dose of .05 mg. The use of 5-HTP at night may eliminate the need for direct melatonin supplementation.

Proteolytic plant enzymes: Include papain (from the papaya) and bromelain (from the pineapple). Bromelain reduces inflammation and swelling. They should form the foundation of anti-inflammatory treatment and be used for pain and fibromyalgia (with CoQ_{10}) in particular and used away from food. When used with food, they are digestive aids.

CONTRAINDICATIONS

Because proteolytic enzymes and essential fatty acids can act as blood thinners, people on blood thinners may need to adjust their doses under the guidance of their health provider.

SYMPTOM-SPECIFIC PROTOCOLS

The following combinations of vitamins, minerals, glandulars, and special nutrients may be added to your core protocol as appropriate:

ADHD
- Borage oil   500–1,000 mg/day
- L-tyrosine   500 mg/day (adjust downward for children)

Alcohol Addiction Recovery
- Adrenal glandular   200 mg, 3 x day
- Hypothalamus glandular   500 mg, 3 x day
- Niacinamide   500 mg, 3 x day
- Magnesium   400–1,200 mg/day
- Potassium   99 mg/day
- Lithium orotate   45 mg/day
- Tryptophan   500 mg, at night
- Melatonin   0.5–1 mg, before bed
- Phenibut (if anxiety)   250–500 mg/day
- Phosphatidylcholine   800–1,200 mg/day
- SAMe   400 mg/day

Anorexia Recovery
- Chromium   600–1,000 mcg
- Vitamin E   400 IU/day
- Vitamin K   1,000 mcg/day
- Beta-carotene   25,000 mg/day

- Potassium   99 mg/day
- Zinc   25 mg/day
- Tyrosine   500 mg/day
- Inositol   1,000–3,000 mg, 2 x day
- SAMe   400 mg/day

Anxiety
- Magnesium threonate   100-400 mg, 3 x day
- Phenibut   250-500 mg/day
- Orthophosphoric acid   30 drops in the morning
                                   (for 1 month)

Bipolar
- Lithium orotate   20 mg, 3 x day
- Chromium   400 mcg/day
- Inositol   4–20 g/day

Blood Glucose Handling and Reactive Hypoglycemia
- B-complex vitamins and minerals
- Chromium   200–400 mcg/day
- Adrenal   100–300 mg/day
- Hypothalamus glandular   1000–6000 mg/day

Bulimia Recovery
- Glucose tolerance factor   600–1,000 mcg/day
- Vitamin B_6 50–100 mg/day
- Magnesium threonate   100–400 mg/day
- Zinc   25 mg, 2 x day.
- 5-HTP   50 mg, 3 x day
- Lactium   150–300 mg/day
- Inositol   2,000 mg, 3 x day
- Whey protein   2 heaping tbsp/day

Chronic Stress and Post-traumatic Stress
- Phosphatidylserine   400 mg/day
- Lactium (De-Stress™)   150–450 mg/day

- Adrenal glandular   250 mg/day
- Hypothalamus glandular   250 mg/day

Note: If high blood pressure w/PTSD, add the following:

- Taurine   500/mg/day

Cognitive Function
- CoQ_{10} 300–600 mg/day
- B_{12} (methylcobalamin)   5,000 mcg/day
- Acetyl L-carnitine   850 mg/day
- CDP-choline   300–1,000 mg/day
- Phosphatidylserine   300 mg/day
- RNA/DNA   200–400 mg/day
- Huperzine A   50–200 mcg/day
- Vinpocetine   10–20 mg/day
- Pregnenolone   50 mg/day.
- Curcumin   80 mg/day
- R–lipoic acid   200 mg/day.
- Brain glandular   250 mg, 2 x day
- Hypothalamus glandular   500 mg, 3 x day

Depression
- B_{12} (methylcobalamin)   1,000 mcg
- 5-HTP   50–150 mg/day
- Adrenal glandular   250 mg, 2 x day before 3 pm
- Borage oil or black currant oil   1,000 mg/day
- Lithium orotate   20 mg/day

For depression, remember to obtain bright light exposure in the morning and to use blue light blocking glasses at least 1–2 hours before going to bed at night.

Insomnia and Sleep Disruption
The most important supplements to regulate circadian rhythm and aid sleep are as follows:

- Lithium orotate   15 mg/day
- Melatonin   0.5 mg, before bed
- Phosphatidylserine   200 mg /day
- Vitamin B$_{12}$ (methylcobalamin)   1,000–2,000 mcg/day (sublingual)
- Magnesium threonate   100–200 mg, before bed
- Lactium (De-Stress™)   150–450 mg, before bed

Pain and Inflammation

A comprehensive enzyme formula that includes proteolytic enzymes:

- Vitamin E   400 IU
- R–alpha lipoic acid   100–200mg/day
- CoQ$_{10}$ 200 mg/day

Panic

- Glycine (strips)   2 g (sublingual), every few
                                                 minutes until attack subsides
- Orthophosphoric acid   30 drops in the morning
                                                 (for 1–2 months)

CHECKLIST FOR NUTRITIONAL SUPPLEMENTATION

- Educate yourself about the role of nutritional supplementation in your overall well-being.
- Prioritize your core nutrients and identify what you will obtain from supplements versus foods (e.g., probiotics supplements or fresh fermented foods—or both).
- Begin with the core nutrients and then add a new nutrient, adding new nutrients only one at a time.
- Apply the drug/nutrient interactions database as you design your protocol.
- Consider whether you need to consult with a nutritional therapist or prescribing clinician.
- Identify obstacles or challenges to adhering to a nutrient protocol.

A Note From the Author: Happy Eating!

I hope your journey though the Good Mood Kitchen is just beginning. Now that you have explored a variety of ideas and methods to give you the power to find your own individual balance, you are ready to put into practice mood-savvy food preparation and nutrition, creating and enjoying simple meals that satisfy complex tastes and desires while healing the brain, mind, and body. You are equipped with numerous choices for foods and nutritional supplementation in your toolbox, so I encourage you to explore your specific bio-individuality. Most importantly, the methods you've learned are designed for you to start anywhere that feels right to you and helps you achieve a healthy response. Follow your gut. Do what feels easy and doable—what excites you and makes you feel energized. Which recipes do you want to try first? What will you prepare for your next dinner party?

As you relinquish fast foods that are designed to be addictive, you will notice increased energy and focus. Don't be afraid to experiment with your own intuitive style of cooking. The Good Mood Kitchen presented in this book is not a static prescription—it is always changing, and no two kitchens are exactly the same. Yours will continue to grow with you as you nourish your own good mood, your way, with the bounty of nature's foods. Happy eating!

Resources

The resources below are those that I have used personally and professionally, or that I am familiar with and represent what I consider high quality resources for your next steps toward mood-savvy wellness. Some of these resources require a licensed clinician to access and some are for you to use directly or to share with your personal clinician. If you do not have a clinician available, you may contact our office for a referral.

Some of these resources offer readers of this book a discount coupon code which may be found here or on Dr. Korn's website at drlesliekorn.com

Where to Obtain High-Quality Nutritional Supplements

Below is a small selection of sources for high-quality nutritional supplements that are often available through professional practitioners or may be ordered online.

Biotics Research Corp
Excellent source of vitamins, minerals, and glandulars, especially the following: Bioglycozyme, De-Stress, LiZyme forte, PT/HPT, Liquid Zinc, Beta Plus and Beta TCP (Beta Plus is designed to support gallbladder function and may be used if the gall bladder has been removed), Amino Acid Quik Sorb, Intenzyme forte, and Proteolytic enzymes.
Website: http://bioticsnw.com/
Address: PO Box 7027, Olympia, WA 98507
Phone: (360) 438-3600

Allergy Research Group
Excellent source of vitamins, minerals, and glandulars—especially free amino acids and glandulars.
Toll-free: (800) 545-9960
Website: http://www.allergyresearchgroup.com/

Carlson Labs
Excellent source for full spectrum vitamin E (EGems) and fish oil.
Website: http://www.carlsonlabs.com/

Integrative Therapeutics
For intestinal support: Glutamine forte, Probiotic pearls
Website: http://www.integrativepro.com/

Nordic Naturals
High-quality fish oil combinations for all ages.
Website: https://www.nordicnaturals.com/

Standard Process
Excellent source of chlorophyll and glandulars.
Website: https://www.standardprocess.com/

Thorne Research
Website: https://thorne.com/

Sources of High-Quality Glandular Supplements
- Biotics Research, Inc
- Standard Process Inc
- Allergy Research, Inc

Where to Obtain Assessments, Testing, and Lab Tests
Many labs listed below require that a licensed professional order the tests for you. However, anyone can order a test through Life Extension Lab.

Life Extension
Provides requisitions for client-ordered blood tests for a variety of markers, including inflammatory markers, homocysteine, HBa1C, hormones, high-

sensitivity C-reactive protein (CRP), fibrinogen, and micronutrient tests (blood).
Website: http://www.lef.org/Vitamins-Supplements/Blood-Tests

Diagnos-Techs

Provides saliva testing for evaluating stress, hormone-related disease, food allergies, gastrointestinal health, 24-hr. Cortisol Test to evaluate HPA axis function, and other health conditions.
Website: http://www.diagnostechs.com/Pages/Intro.aspx

Gluten and Food Allergy/Food Sensitivity Testing

Cyrex™ specializes in testing for autoimmune conditions.
Website: https://www.cyrexlabs.com/
Tests: https://www.cyrexlabs.com/CyrexTestsArrays/tabid/136/Default.aspx

The Mediator Release Test

Tests for food- and food-chemical-induced inflammation.
Website: http://nowleap.com/mediator-release-testing/the-patented-mediator-release-test-mrt/

SpectraCell

Provides nutritional testing, including MTHFR, telomere testing, micronutrient tests (blood), and nutrient status for physicians and their clients. SpectraCell Labs also conducts telomere testing via blood sample submission.
Website: http://www.spectracell.com/

BodySync

DNA test for 45 variables that affect nutritional and fitness status.
Website: https://bodysync.com/tests.aspx

Trace Elements

Provides hair tissue mineral analysis for metabolic type, mineral ratios, and heavy metals.
Website: http://www.traceelements.com/

For Further Study About Mental Health Nutrition

Dr. Leslie Korn's NutriPsych Training Program: Mental Health Nutrition and cooking courses from beginner to advanced and practitioner level (all levels) Also, the Brainbow Blueprint, a course on food, nutrition, and mental health developed for everyone.

Website: drlesliekorn.com

Seminars

Integrative Treatments for Mental Health: Practical Evidence-Based Solutions for Depression, Anxiety, Insomnia and Eating Disorders, with Dr. Leslie Korn

This 7-hour continuing education DVD provides a comprehensive overview of nutritional therapies for mental health and their integration with other modalities.

Beyond Fish Oil: 10 Dietary Strategies to Improve and Balance Mood

A 2 Hour nutrition and cooking video

Website: https://catalog.pesi.com/speaker/leslie-korn-7125

Nutritional Therapy Practitioner Program (NTP)

This distance-learning program provides students with 9 months of distance training with the flexibility of self-paced study, teleconference calls, and three separate multiple-day, instructor-led workshops during the 15-module course.

Website: http://nutritionaltherapy.com/ntt-programs/ntp-classes/

Saybrook University Integrative and Functional Nutrition Certificate and Graduate Degree

Website: https://www.saybrook.edu/academics/certificate-programs/ integrative-and-functional-nutrition-certificate/

Maryland University Graduate Degree in Nutrition and Integrative Health

Website: http://www.muih.edu/academics/masters-degrees/ master-science-nutrition-integrative-health

Weston A. Price Foundation
Provides education, research, and activism for restoring nutrient-dense foods to the human diet. Annual conference.
Website: http://www.westonaprice.org/

Finding Clinical, Coaching and Professional Support
Health Coaches
Providing coaching for clinicians and clients who want to improve their mental and physical well being though nutrition and other natural medicine methods
Website: drlesliekorn.com

Integrative Nutrition
Website: http://www.integrativenutrition.com/career/healthcoaching

National Consortium for Credentialing Health & Wellness Coaches
Website: http://www.ncchwc.org/

Duke University Health Coach Program
Website: http://www.dukeintegrativemedicine.org/patient-care/
   integrative-health-coaching

Nutritional Counselors/Therapists
Nutritional Therapy Association
Website: http://nutritionaltherapy.com/

The National Association of Nutrition Professionals
Website: http://nanp.org/

Registered Dietitians
To find a functional and integrative dietitian in your area, go to the website for the Academy of Nutrition and Dietetics.
Website: https://integrativerd.org/

Naturopathic Physicians
American Association of Naturopathic Physicians
Website: www.naturopathic.org

Functional Medicine Practitioners
Institute for Functional Medicine
Website: www.functionalmedicine.org

Integrative Medical Practitioners
The American Board of Integrative Holistic Medicine (ABIHM)
Website: http://www.abihm.org

Databases

My Nutrition Advisor: Online free and paid subscription resource
for nutrition, and purchase of high quality, easy to make "smoothie
packs." Use the code korn for a 5% discount on products.
Website: https://mynutritionadvisor.com

Drug-Nutrient Interactions Online Database
Use this database to enter a drug or supplement; you can then receive a full
interaction report that includes notice of potential interactions.
Mailing address: Integrative Therapeutics, LLC, 825 Challenger Drive
Green Bay, WI 54311
Phone: 800-931-1709
Website: http://www.integrativepro.com/Resources/
Drug-Nutrient-Interaction-Checker

Nutrition Data
Detailed nutrition information, plus unique analysis tools that tell you
more about how foods affect your health and make it easier to choose
healthy foods.
Website: http://nutritiondata.self.com/

RxISK
RxISK is a free and independent website where patients, doctors, and phar-
macists can research prescription drugs and easily report a drug side effect.
Website: https://rxisk.org/

Foods and Food-Related Technologies
Bragg's Apple Cider Vinegar
Organic raw apple cider vinegar.

Phone (toll-free): 800-446-1990
E-mail: General information: info@bragg.com
Website: http://www.bragg.com/

Find Real Food App
An app that lists over 13,000 researched foods and brands highest in nutrient density, without additives and processing.
Website: http://www.findrealfoodapp.com/

HAPIfork
The HAPIfork is an electronic fork that helps you monitor and track your eating habits.
Website: http://www.hapi.com/

Salt Fire & Time
If you do not have time to make your own broth, or just want to taste another medicinal broth, these two sisters make the best broth, and they will ship.
Website: saltfireandtime.com
Address: 115 NE 6th Ave, Portland, OR 97232
Phone: 503-208-2758

Vibrant Blue Oils.
High quality culinary and aromatherapy essential oils specializing in mental wellness.
Use code goodmood to receive 10% discount on purchases.
Website: https://vibrantblueoils.com

Cooking Skills
Cooking Matters
Helps families to shop for and cook healthy meals on a budget.
Address: 1030 15th Street NW, Suite 1100, Washington DC, 20005
Website: http://cookingmatters.org/

Food Scores App
Produced by Environmental Working Group, this app rates the quality of the food/brand name and produces an overall score between 1 and 10.
Website: http://www.ewg.org/foodscores?inlist=Y&sdf=1

Knife Skill Video Techniques–HD
This HD video series teaches the basics of how to work with knives and also has tutorials on how to sharpen your knife, and on butchery.
Website: http://www.stellaculinary.com/knife-skill-video-techniques-hd

Cookbooks/Blogs

These resources are among the best food cookbooks and blogs. Watch out for use of some ingredients like sugar that you will want to avoid. Just make a substitution.

NomNom Paleo
A fun recipe-rich blog and resource for food prep for health.
Website: http://nomnompaleo.com/

Canal Street Cooking
Website: http://thecanalhouse.com/

Food52
Website: http://food52.com/

Kitchen Appliances

Blender
Brands to look for include Vitamix, K-Tec Blender, Juiceman Smoothies, and Tribest Blender.

Juicer
Champion Juicer is a very high-quality juicer.
Website: http://championjuicer.com/

Dehydrator
The Excalibur is a good choice for a dehydrator, as it has temperature control, is fan-operated, and is easy to clean.
Website: http://www.excaliburdehydrator.com/

Colors of the "Brainbow"

Color	Foods	Nutrients	Benefits
Red	Cherries Cranberries Red cabbage Beets Radicchio Tomatoes Red onions Red bell peppers Red kidney beans Pink grapefruit Red potatoes Rhubarb Red apples and pears Rainbow chard Red grapes Strawberries Raspberries Radishes Red chilies Watermelon	Lycopene (tomatoes, watermelon, pink grapefruit) Anthocyanins (strawberries, raspberries, red grapes) Antioxidants (cherries, cranberries, proanthocyanidins) Anti-inflammatory Vitamin C (red bell peppers, beets, strawberries, tomatoes) Vitamin A (beets, tomatoes) Betaine (beets) Vitamin K (beets) Folate (beets) Quercetin Hesperidin	Improves memory Improves digestion Improves heart health Lowers blood pressure
Orange	Carrots Sweet potatoes Oranges Peaches Pumpkins Apricots Cantaloupe Mangoes Papaya Tangerines Butternut squash Nectarines	Antioxidants (sweet potatoes) Beta-carotene (sweet potatoes, pumpkins, carrots) Vitamin A (peaches, sweet potatoes) Folate (oranges) Vitamin C (peaches, sweet potatoes, oranges) Iron (sweet potatoes) Carotenoids Bioflavonoids Fiber Magnesium (oranges)	Improves digestion Boosts immunity Prevents cellular damage Promotes healthy mucous membranes

Color	Foods	Nutrients	Benefits
Yellow	Yellow bell peppers Lemons Corn Bananas (also white) Pineapple Yellow squash (butterstick, acorn, delicata) Yellow apples and pears Yellow tomatoes	Alpha-carotene Beta-carotene Anthoxanthins Bromelain (pineapple) Carotenoids (yellow peppers) Vitamin A (yellow peppers) Vitamin C (pineapple, yellow peppers)	Improves brain function Improves digestion Boosts immunity
Green	Cucumbers Leeks Brussels sprouts Arugula Asparagus Kiwi Lettuce Green bell peppers Kale Pumpkin seeds Lima beans Spinach Chard Broccoli Peas Zucchini Green cabbage Green apples	Antioxidants (spinach) Lutein (spinach, dark leafy greens, green peppers, cucumber, peas, celery) Indoles (broccoli, cabbage) Folate (kiwi) Glutathione (kiwi) Vitamin E (kiwi) Vitamin C (kale) Calcium (broccoli) Iron (broccoli, spinach, pumpkin seeds, peas, lima beans, kale) Folate (spinach, broccoli) Vitamin A (kale) Vitamin K (spinach, kale) Chlorophyll Calcium (kale)	Detoxification, oxidative stress reduction, improves brain function and liver function
Blue/ Purple	Blueberries Eggplant Blackberries Plums Currants Elderberries Purple grapes Purple carrots Purple cabbage Purple kale Purple potatoes	Anthocyanin (blueberries) Antioxidants (blackberries, blueberries) Fiber Flavonoids Vitamin B (plums) Vitamin E (blueberries) Vitamin C (blueberries, eggplant) Vitamin K (blackberries, plums) Calcium (eggplant) Phosphorus (eggplant)	Improves memory Improves circulation Boosts brain activity Boosts immunity Improves digestion Improves blood sugar regulation

Color	Foods	Nutrients	Benefits
White	Garlic Onions Cauliflower Potatoes Turnips Jicama Bananas (also yellow) White corn Parsnips Mushrooms Jerusalem artichokes White peaches White nectarines White radishes White beans	Antimicrobial (garlic, onions) Quercetin (onions) Manganese (cauliflower) Vitamin C (cauliflower) Protein (white beans) Iron (white beans) Potassium (white beans, bananas) Vitamin B_6 (garlic)	Reduces blood pressure Boosts immunity Cellular protection and recovery New cell growth, circulation, detoxification Lowers blood sugar
Black	Black wild rice Black beans Black lentils	Protein (black rice) Antioxidants/anthocyanins (black rice, black lentils, black beans) Copper (black rice)	Detoxification Balances cholesterol levels Prevention of Alzheimer's and diabetes

Don't eat foods containing these additives!

High fructose corn syrup

Aspartame

Hydrolyzed protein

Autolyzed yeast

Monosodium glutamate (MSG)

Potassium bromate (flours and baked goods)

Brominated vegetable oil, or BVO (citrus flavorings in sports drinks)

BHA and BHT (found in breakfast cereals, snack foods, gum, pies, cakes, and processed meats)

Trans fats

Artificial colors

Enriched wheat

Hydrogenated or fractionated oils

Sugar

Potassium benzoate and sodium benzoate (apple cider, salad dressing, jams, pickled foods)

Acesulfame-K

Sucralose

Propyl gallate (meat products, chicken soup base, gum)

Sodium chloride

Soy and soy lecithin

Corn

Polysorbate 80

Canola oil

Shopping List for Good Mood Recipes

Organic Oils and Fats	✓
Avocado oil	
Coconut cream or milk	
Coconut oil	
Flax seed oil	
Ghee	
Hemp oil	
Raw grass-fed butter	
Toasted sesame oil	
Virgin olive oil	

Herbs and Spices	✓
Basil, fresh and dried	
Bay leaves	
Black pepper (freshly ground)	
Black mustard seeds	
Caraway seeds	
Cardamom, ground	
Cardamom pods	
Cayenne	
Cilantro	
Cinnamon, ground	

Herbs and Spices	✓
Cinnamon sticks	
Cloves	
Coriander powder	
Curry Powder	
Cumin, seeds and ground	
Dill, fresh and dried	
Fennel seeds	
Fenugreek seeds	
Garlic, fresh and dried	
Ginger, fresh and dried	
Kelp powder	
Nutmeg	
Oregano, fresh and dried	
Parsley, fresh and dried	
Red pepper flakes	
Rosemary, fresh and dried	
Saffron	
Sea salt, gray and pink	
Spearmint, fresh	
Tarragon, fresh and dried	
Thyme	
Turmeric, fresh and dried	
Vanilla beans	
Vanilla extract	

Vegetables	✓
Arugula	
Beets	
Broccoli	
Carrots	
Cabbage (green, napa, red)	
Cauliflower	
Celery	
Cucumber	
Kale	
Lettuce	
Mushrooms (shiitake or button)	
Nopal cactus	
Onion	
Peapods	
Potatoes	
Red bell pepper	
Scallions	
Shallots	
Snow peas	
Spinach	
Sprouts	
Sweet potatoes	
Swiss chard	

Proteins	✓
Bacon	
Beef	
Canned wild salmon	
Chicken, organic	
Dried cod (bacalao, in Spanish)	
Dried green peas	
Farm-raised grass-fed eggs	
Farm-raised organic chicken livers	
Fresh wild salmon	
Gelatin	
Organic sausages	
Pickled herring	
Red, brown, or green lentils	
Sardines in olive oil	
Smoked salmon	
Split yellow mung dahl beans	
Tofu	
Tuna (preservative free)	
Turkey	
Wild shrimp	
White beans	
Dairy options	
Goat cheeses	
Heavy cream	

Grains	✓
Almond flour	
Buckwheat flour	
Couscous	
Millet	
Quinoa	
Rice (Arborio, black, brown, white)	
Rice flour	
Tapioca flour	

Raw Nuts and Seeds	✓
Almonds	
Cashews	
Chia seeds	
Hazelnuts/Filberts	
Flax seed	
Peanuts (limit to special occasions)	
Pecans	
Sesame seeds	
Pumpkin seeds	
Sunflower seeds	
Walnuts	

Nut/Seed Butters	✓
Almond	
Cashew	
Tahini	

Fruits (fresh, frozen, and dried)	✓
Apple	
Avocado	
Banana	
Blueberry	
Cherries	
Coconut, shredded	
Cranberry	
Currants	

Fruits (fresh, frozen, and dried)	✓
Figs	
Lemon	
Lime	
Mango	
Orange	
Pineapple	
Raspberries	
Raisins	
Watermelon	

Beverages	✓
Black tea, green tea	
Coffee	
Chai	
Non-dairy milk (almond, coconut, hemp)	
Organic decaf coffee	
Rooibos tea	

Sweeteners	✓
Agave (Dark, unrefined)	
Maple syrup (B-grade)	
Raw honey	
Stevia liquid	

Glossary of Key Terms

allergen. A substance like dust, animal dander, or certain foods like seafood or nuts, exposure to which causes a reaction in the immune system. The immune system thinks it is being attacked by an invader and "fights off the threat," which leads to the symptoms we know as "allergies."

ancestral diets. Foods, diets, and preparation methods that have been used by our ancestors for millennia. They are foods to which our ancestors' bodies evolved, in their particular geographic regions, to optimize nourishment. The traditional ancestral nutrition approach to mental health—also called authentic nutrition—suggests that in order to achieve health and well-being, mentally and physically, we should eat the types of foods that are most similar to the foods our ancestors ate.

blood sugar. A colloquial term for *blood glucose.* It refers to sugar that is carried via the bloodstream to supply energy to the cells in the body. Blood sugar needs to be in balance to maintain optimal mood regulation, and this balance is in turn regulated primarily by the hormone *insulin.* Blood glucose rises and falls throughout the day in response to food intake (or the absence thereof) and factors such as stress. When blood glucose rises too high and stays high, over time it becomes *diabetes type 2.* Blood sugar that rapidly swings high and then low before and after meals is called *functional hypoglycemia.*

body clock. Our 24-hour sleep-wake cycle, which is governed by the light and dark cycle of the day and night. This body clock governs rhythms of stress hormones and has a significant influence on mood and physical and emotional well-being.

brainbow diet. My term for a full-color-spectrum diet that nourishes the brain, mind, and body in order to enhance mental health.

casein. The protein found in dairy milk products. Both gluten and casein contain proteins to which people may be either allergic or sensitive. About 50% of people who are sensitive to gluten are sensitive to casein. This is called *cross-reactivity*. Eliminating casein is a central component to nutritional treatment of autism.

cholesterol. A waxy, fat-like substance that is required for the production of hormones, including vitamin D. Twenty-five percent of the cholesterol in the body is found in the brain, and it is a requirement for healthy brain function. Often considered a contributor to vascular and heart disease, cholesterol levels are all-too-frequently misunderstood and erroneously treated with medications and low-fat diets.

comfort foods. Foods that provide comfort for emotional or physical distress. While comfort foods may differ for each individual, they are commonly comprised of starchy carbohydrates or sugar-rich foods and combined with high-fat foods. These foods are often mood-sedating. However, we can also choose to prepare comfort foods that provide both comfort and health by using healthy ingredients for mental and physical nourishment.

community-supported agriculture (CSA). A network of local individuals who agree to work and share cooperatively in the growing and/or purchase of farm-raised products. It represents a cost-effective way to grow and obtain healthy organic foods. CSAs are found worldwide.

detoxification. The process by which the body eliminates toxins generated by digestion or due to exposure to external toxins. The liver is the main organ of detoxification and is aided by specific foods such as garlic, onions, and the cruciferous vegetables (broccoli, cauliflower). Nutrients and specific types of fasting also help detoxify the body. Detoxification methods and rituals are found across all cultures.

diet. The complete list of food and nutritional choices we make to nourish our brain, mind, and body. Some diets provide this nourishment much more effectively than others.

digestion. The process by which foods are broken down into smaller particles, through mechanical (chewing and peristalsis) and enzymatic (digestive enzymes and acids) methods, so they can be absorbed in the bloodstream and used throughout the body. Digestion releases the nutrients in food so that the body can use them efficiently.

fast food. Food that is mass-produced, usually inexpensive, and most often comprised of very poor-quality proteins, fats, and refined carbohydrates, all of which lead to chronic inflammation and mental and physical illness. Fast food is often made with large quantities of salt and sugar, in part as a deliberate way to enhance its addictive nature.

fiber. The part of a plant/vegetable/fruit that cannot be digested. Two kinds of fiber are found in various degrees in different foods—*soluble* and *insoluble*—and both are essential for good health and healthy digestion. Eating plenty of vegetables, fruits, seeds, and nuts ensures enough fiber intake to cleanse and "scrub" the intestines and provide bulk for healthy elimination from the colon.

food addiction. Lack of control in choosing to eat certain types and quantities of foods. It often involves intense cravings for refined carbohydrates, including sugar, flour, fats, and salt. Food addiction is rooted in brain chemistry and the effects of refined substances, which act like powerful drugs in our brains. Addressing food addiction involves withdrawal from these substances, the substitution of satisfying alternatives that nourish the brain, mind, and body, and adjusting behavioral habits toward healthier ways to satisfy the basic needs that underlie our cravings.

food combination. The concept that certain types of foods digest better when combined so as not to compete for different enzymes. For example, a combination of proteins and starches is to be avoided, while proteins and green vegetables digest well together. Fruits are best eaten alone. Combining foods in a more mindful and informed way can be particularly helpful for those who experience gas or chronic indigestion. It may also be considered a simplified approach to diet.

food-mood connection. The concept that food has an effect on mood. Certain foods like refined foods can contribute to depressed moods and other foods can stabilize or elevate mood. The effects of food on mood derive from a variety of influences including blood glucose, fat intake, metabolism, neurotransmitter synthesis, and inflammation.

food sensitivities. Also called *food intolerance*, and often incorrectly referred to as *food allergies*, food sensitivities arise from exposure to a variety of foods and may lead to an innate or an acquired reaction or symptom.

glucose balance. Also called *blood sugar regulation*, this is the process by which the body maintains the relative balance of blood glucose required to properly fuel the brain and organs of the body. Blood glucose changes in response to food intake and the complex metabolic interplay between the liver, pancreas, and adrenal glands throughout the day. Reactive hypoglycemia and diabetes type 2 reflect the failure of the body to balance glucose.

gluten. The protein found in certain grains (wheat, barley, and rye) that causes grains to "glue" together. Gliadins are proteins that are components of gluten. Celiac disease is an autoimmune hereditary allergy to gluten that affects about 1 in 250 people. It manifests in severe digestive symptoms, and frequently in neurological symptoms. Non-celiac gluten sensitivity is an intolerance leading to both digestive and neurological problems. It may or may not manifest in digestive distress and often goes undiagnosed.

hypoglycemia. Also called *reactive hypoglycemia*, a condition in which a person's blood glucose (sugar) levels fall too low after eating, often within 4 hours or less. Hypoglycemia can cause dizziness, fatigue, sleepiness, irritability, or even rage. It is often a precursor to diabetes type 2 if not addressed. Eating good-quality foods, avoiding eating sugars or refined foods, stress reduction, and nutritional supplementation all support recovery from hypoglycemia.

individualized nutrition. Foods and supplements that are tailored to the bio-cultural and genetic needs of an individual rather than being based on fads or ideologies. Individualized diets range from vegetarian to carnivore. Some nutritional supplements may be indicated, while others are shown to be detrimental for a particular individual.

inflammation. The body's natural response in order to heal an injury. Ongoing injurious exposures from poor-quality oils, pesticides, heavy metals, and air pollution lead to low-level inflammation that can result in chronic illness. Using nutritional anti-inflammatories and avoiding injurious foods protects against chronic inflammation.

lactose. A sugar that is present in dairy products. Deficiency in the enzyme that digests lactose leads to intolerance. Some people with lactose intolerance may be able to tolerate dairy products that have a higher fat content, such as pure cream or butter, because the lactose content is lower in these products. Many processed foods contain lactose, so it is important for those with lactose intolerance to always read food labels to check for milk, lactose, whey, curds, dry milk solids, nonfat dry milk powder, and milk by-products.

leaky gut. An increase in normal intestinal permeability, which allows substances to leak into the bloodstream, resulting in illness. Leaky gut can arise from gluten, dairy, and other food sensitivities, as well as candida overgrowth or infectious processes.

long-term nutritional change. The process of changing one's habits, behaviors and food choices to improve overall well-being. Nutritional changes often occur over time through experimenting with what enhances or detracts from one's health.

metabolism. The conversion of food into energy. Each person has a rate of metabolism determined by genetic heritage. Metabolism can be altered to some degree by food choices and exercise patterns, and it also responds to acute or chronic illness.

nightshades. Members of the Solanaceae plant family, including tomatoes, potatoes (excluding sweet potatoes and yams), eggplant, and peppers (excluding black pepper). Symptoms of nightshade sensitivity include muscle pain and tightness, arthritis, sensitivity to weather changes, morning stiffness, slow healing, gallbladder problems, heartburn, and GERD.

nutritional supplementation. Although a healthy diet is essential for mental health, it is not generally sufficient to treat mental illness. Vitamins, minerals, amino acids, special nutrients, and glandulars are also necessary. They are contained in foods and supplements and alter the biochemistry of our brain, mind, and body. The effective use of these resources depends upon an individualized approach. These supplements are essential to restoring mental wellness and reducing or eliminating psychotropic medications. Nutritional supplementation should always be carried out with caution, ideally in collaboration with a licensed professional.

oxidation. The rate at which we burn carbohydrates, or glucose. Some of us burn carbohydrates more quickly, and some burn them more slowly. People can be divided into three general body categories: the *fast oxidizers,* whose blood pH tends toward a little more acid and who are typically carnivores; the *slow oxidizers,* whose blood pH tends to be more alkaline and who do better on more plant proteins; and the *mixed or balanced oxidizers,* who do well with a mix of carbohydrates, proteins, and fats. What foods/fuel mix we require is determined by our genetics, just like the color of our eyes, our height, or our blood type.

prebiotics. Soluble, indigestible dietary fibers that support beneficial gut microbiota (bacteria) that live in the colon. Foods containing prebiotics include onions, garlic, Jerusalem artichokes, leeks, asparagus, wheat, beans, bananas, agave, dandelion, chicory root, and chia.

principle of substitutions. Foods we crave provide chemical reactions that the brain/mind wants and needs. The key to overcoming these food addictions is to understand one's unique "craving" profile and interpret the foods one craves, and when, to understand the emotional biochemistry of the foods, identify the need they satisfy, and find substitutions that address these needs without the negative side effects and detrimental health effects. This is the "principle of substitutions"—finding an alternative food to provide the same effect by substituting a healthy food or substance for a less healthy one.

probiotics. Healthy bacteria that help to lower the stress response by regulating relaxation-related neurotransmitters in the brain. Probiotics may be bought in capsule or liquid form in a health food store and are also found in fermented foods.

refined carbohydrates. Sugars and starches that have been extracted from whole foods and repackaged into highly addictive substances. Examples include white flour, white sugar, and corn syrup.

second brain. The intestinal tract—or the gut—often called the "second brain" because it is a major source of neurotransmitter production in the body.

simplified diet. The practice of choosing simple whole foods in small increments in order to eliminate potential offenders that contribute to allergies, sensitives, or inflammation; to give the body a rest; and to restore mental and emotional wellbeing. Simplified diets include the *elimination diet*, a systematic elimination over weeks and months of potential foods that contribute to leaky gut and physical and neurological symptoms; the *anti-inflammatory diet*, which targets foods that can cause inflammation in the body, like nightshades and vegetable oils; the *carnivore diet*, also called *paleo*, which focuses on animal proteins and fats and excludes grains and dairy; the *vegetarian diet*, a high-carbohydrate diet of vegetables, fruits, nuts, legumes, grains, and fats derived from plants; the *balanced spectrum diet*, which is ideal for individuals who will do well on all types of whole, nutrient-dense foods and which includes a balance of animal and plant proteins, fats, grains, and legumes; and the *brainbow diet*—a diet attuned to each individual's specific genetic and cultural needs to support brain, mind, and body function, with a focus on foods from the whole color spectrum.

standard American diet (SAD). This too-frequently followed diet consists of refined, overly processed foods containing refined sugars in fruit juices and sugary drinks, and highly refined rice, pastas, and flours in breads and bakery goods. These processed products are loaded with chemicals and synthetic preservatives, hormones, antibiotics, and food colorings that are known to alter our mood. The standard American diet leads to chronic inflammatory states and sets the stage for neurotransmitter imbalances. The SAD diet makes us sad because it does not provide the nutrients our brain and body need to function well.

substance use. The use of any kind of substance that alters brain, mind, body, and/or consciousness with either a positive (healthy) or negative (unhealthy) effect. May include drugs, alcohol, and/or foods, and can involve addiction as well as non-addicted ritual behaviors.

toxins. Mental health is affected negatively by dietary exposure to food toxins and allergens. It is important to eliminate from your diet any food that contains additives, preservatives, hormones, toxic pesticides, and petrochemical fertilizers. They're more common than you might think! Commonly encountered toxin types include neurotoxins, food additives and preservatives, heavy metals, and environmental toxins in the home and kitchen.

Index

Recipe Index

About the Author

Leslie Korn, PhD, MPH, is a clinician, educator, speaker, and health coach specializing in mental health nutrition and integrative medicine. She is author of the celebrated *Nutrition Essentials for Mental Health*, which is a comprehensive guide to integrating the power of nutritional change in clinical practice, and other books, articles, and mental health cookbooks. A core faculty member of Capella University's Mental Health Counseling and doctoral studies Program, Dr. Korn has been a Clinical Fellow at Harvard Medical School, conducted research in nutrition at the Harvard School of Public Health, served as a Fulbright scholar in traditional medicine, and a National Institutes of Health-funded research scientist in mind-body medicine. In 1975 she founded the Center for Traditional Medicine, a public health natural medicine clinic in rural indigenous Mexico that she has directed for over 40 years. She teaches and consults internationally for mental health professionals, clients, popular audiences, and tribal communities.